# Poems
## by
# *Marines*
## in Combat

## Nancie Saxton

*To David,*

*Thank you for your services & may God bless you always,*

*Nancie*

"Many of the poems from World War I through The Gulf War are intense, others are whimsical".
—*The Charlotte Tribune*

*I dedicate this book to*
*all the Marines that have fought for our freedom.*
*With a special dedication to the two Marines who*
*have been a special part of my life,*
*my loving father,*
*Sergeant Richard E. Saxton, 1951-1953 Korea,*
*and*
*Corporal Michael P. Prikril, 1968-1971 Vietnam.*

AuthorHouse™
1663 Liberty Drive
Bloomington, IN 47403
www.authorhouse.com
Phone: 1-800-839-8640

First published by AuthorHouse    9/15/2010

ISBN: 978-1-4520-5800-9 (sc)
ISBN: 978-1-4520-5801-6 (hc)
ISBN: 978-1-4520-5802-3 (e)

Library of Congress: 2010913633

Printed in the United States of America

This book is printed on acid-free paper.

# ACKNOWLEDGMENTS

Thank you God for everything.

To all the people who sent in poems, I thank you for your contributions to publish in this book. The letters I received along with the poems were always something to look forward to. I will miss them.

Thank you Mom and Dad for all your love, help, and support. Especially these last few years. I never would have been able to make the transition without you both.

Thank you brother Ray for all your love, help, and support over the years. You're the best brother any girl could ever have.

Thank you Karen for encouraging me to try again to get the book published. Your sisterly support is a great comfort.

Thank you Mike Prikril for sharing your poems with me and allowing your poems to be my inspiration for this book. Everyone comes into our lives for a reason.

Thank you Kim Norris for proof reading this book.

Thank you Michael Christie for never letting me fall and for always being there whenever I needed you and thank you for all that you have taught me over the years.

# Table of Contents

**Chapter 2—*World War Two*** *(continued)*

**Chapter 4—*Vietnam War***

**Chapter 4—*Vietnam War*** *(continued)*

**Chapter 5—*Gulf War***

**Chapter 6—*Miscellaneous***

**Chapter 6—*Miscellaneous*** *(continued)*

**Chapter 7—*Unknown Authors***

**Corporal, 5th Marine Regiment, France, 1917**
*Artwork by Darko Pavlovic*
*from Men-at-Arms 327: US Marine Corps in World War I 1917–1918*
*© Osprey Publishing*

# WORLD WAR I

## (1917 - 1918)

| Total service members | 4,734,991 |
|---|---|
| Battle deaths | 53,402 |
| Other deaths in service (nontheater) | 63,114 |
| Nonmortal woundings | 204,002 |
| Living veterans (102)[1] | 2,212 |

1. Median ages.

*Source: Department of Defense and Veterans Administration, Sept. 30, 2001.*

# AFTER ARMISTICE
*by: Private Clarence Earle Moullette*
*USMC, 68381,*
*Bellean Wood - Chateau Thierry*
*Marine Cemetery, France, 1919*

"How many more must die, O God?
How many more must lie beneath the sod,
'ere man has learned to live in peace?

"Yea, count not the rancours in their hearts
for have they learned as men of parts
that they may spread their canvas 'neath the dome
of heaven, and call it home.

"We've seen the spread of anguished hands
which threw the torch
that somehow missed the mark, and filled
the earth to scorch
in one vast purging flame, for which
no man would shoulder blame.

"We offer up our prayers to peace
whilst in our hands we hold
the shards of poignant suffering
unto the last. Alas!"

*—5th Marine Regiment*
*4th Marine Brigade*
*2nd Infantry (Army) Division,*
*American Expeditionary Force (AEF)*

**Pfc., 5th Marines, 1st Marine Division; Peleliu, 1944**
*Artwork by Mike Chappell*
*from Elite Series 59: US Marine Corps 1941-45*
© *Osprey Publishing*

# WORLD WAR II

## (1940 - 1945)

| Total service members | 16,112,566 |
|---|---|
| Battle deaths | 291,557 |
| Other deaths in service (nontheater) | 113,842 |
| Nonmortal woundings | 671,846 |
| Living veterans (80)[1] | 5,032,591 |

1. Median ages.

*Source: Department of Defense and Veterans Administration, Sept. 30, 2001.*

## SEMPER FI LOVE
*by: Master Sergeant Carl M. (Bud) DeVere, Sr.*

The wonderful love of a beautiful maid
The love of a staunch, true man
The love of a baby unafraid
Have existed since time began.
But the greatest of loves
The quintessence of loves
Even greater than that of a mother
Is the tender, passionate, infinite love
Of one drunken Marine for another.

## A WORLD WAR II DITTY
*by: Master Sergeant Carl M. (Bud) DeVere, Sr.*

The Marines, the Marines, those blasted Gyrenes,
Those sea-going bellhops, those brass-button queens,
Oh, they pat their own backs, write stories in reams,
All in praise of themselves—the U.S. Marines!

The Marines, the Marines, those publicity fiends,
They built all the forests, turned on all the streams,
Discontent with the earth, they say Heaven's scenes
Are guarded by—you guess—the U.S. Marines!

# THE 'CANAL

*by: Master Sergeant Carl M. (Bud) DeVere, Sr.*

The Tempo of the heart increases so fast,
But it stops all at once with a .25 blast.
Then a "Can" sneaks through and throws in a dud,
A Leatherneck jumps in a puddle of mud.
The .155 shakes the ground. Blood in the foxhole.
Blood all around.

Shrapnel screams, Zeros snort, you see the flash,
Then you hear the report.
The whine of the Grumman, the swish of the shell,
The heat of the tracer is hotter than Hell.
The rumble of the tank is the Devil's own laugh;
Life ebbs away on a downward graph.

The guns of the Japs go "Boomlay, BOOM!"
"Ack Ack" follows with a jungle tune.
The sun comes up on the dead all around.
The trees mostly rest with their trunks on the ground.
In the top of a palm hangs a sniper by his foot,
There's a strafing plane in a pile of soot.

When the dust clears away in a few years more,
And the blood drives up, and there's no more war,
We'll be back in the States with just one thought.
The thought of the lesson that the Solomons taught.

## Glossary for "THE 'CANAL"

Ack Ack —An Anti-aircraft gun, which when fired makes an "Ack Ack" sound.

Can —A Japanese Navy destroyer.

Dud —A round of ammunition which fails to explode when it is designed to. Dangerous because it may go off at any time, or never.

Grumman —Manufacturer of the Marine F4F fighter plane. The plane was the early "work horse" of aerial battle over Guadalcanal, and was fondly referred to as a "Grumman" by ground troops.

Leatherneck —A 1775 nickname for Marines whose uniforms had a leather collar to ward off enemy sword blows in close combat.

Tracer —A bullet which trails fire behind. They are dispersed in a machine gun belt of ammunition. When fired, the flaming rounds give the gunner a visual location of where he is shooting. (Especially at night).

Zero —Designation for a Japanese fighter plane.

.25 Blast —Japanese .25 caliber rifle.

.155 —Nickname of a cannon which fires a .155 millimeter shell.

### IN THE FIELD OF BATTLE
*by: Private First Class Darold W. Powell*
*Winter 1942*

*Submitted by: Glen Miller*


The United States Marines are in action again,
In the Solomon Islands where the battle never ends.
They live like dogs in the mud and sand.
Eating only twice a day and then from a tin can.
The flies are terrible from the bodies that rot,
From the wide blue ocean to the bloody mountaintop.
The fight goes on with patrol after patrol,
And every time they return, there is many a lost soul.


It is war in the Pacific and the Marines must fight,
For the mothers and fathers and all things that are right.
The Jap machine guns rattle and you get close to the deck,
The mortar shells drop and the battle field is a wreck.
It is a mass of dead and wounded Marines.
But the casualties are greater on the yellow fields.
You curse the yellow Japs and then say a prayer,
As you see your buddies falling everywhere.


I would like to get away to a land that is free,
And never have to worry about a sniper in a tree.
Away from the bombs that comes screaming down,
They get louder and louder as they hit the ground.
The motors groan as they spin and dive.
And the bombers explode as a shell burst nearby.
Six bombers and twenty zeros shot all to hell.


*Continued...*

## IN THE FIELD OF BATTLE *(continued)*

What is to happen to this world of ours?
That is being ripped apart by the axis powers.
To stop them our boys must learn to hate and kill.
Our factories must hum and our workers be skilled.
We cannot lose because we are fighting for the right,
And when the allies pull together,
There is going to be a great fight.
When will the fighting and killing end?
And when will the Marines go home again?
Home to the states that they love so well.
Away from Guadalcanal the land of Hell.

## THE MARINES' IMMORTAL ROCK
*by: Edward F. Burke and John Bauer*
*4th Division USMC*
*March 1945*

They fought and won Tripoli and Montezuma too,
At Iwo Jima their Victory cry was heard anew.
I'll remember forever more,
How they landed on that barren shore.

A shell falls here, a shell bursts there,
Marines falling, nevermore to care.
The earth gave up its level look
As the shells their deadly quota took.

The Amtracks were blown to metallic wrecks,
As on they advancd, these Leathernecks.
On to the airport advanced the Fifth,
As we, the Fourth, moved to the cliff.

"Knock out these pillboxes", one did call,
Then Naval gunfire gave its all.
Under continuous bombardment the walls did cave,
Sealing the Japs in a smouldering grave.

Our obstacle removed, our falling Colonel did shout,
"The ridge is ours, Devil Dogs - Move Out."
Darkness has settled ov'r the isle,
Now a Marine has time to think awhile.

*Continued...*

## THE MARINES' IMMORTAL ROCK *(continued)*

This morning's happenings does he recall,
Above all our beloved Chaplain did wounded fall.
Now as if "Old Ruggeds" iron hand touched each man's shoulder,
Again on their feet they moved out much bolder.

As heaven knows, he has played his Holy role,
The men went forward as if their hearts he did control.
Now battle memories from this Marine fade fast,
With thoughts of Mother and Dad he sleeps at last.

Out of the dark night there came a shriek,
By which out of every heart courage did leak.
A sound that no man can describe at its peak,
Yet every human being it did seem to seek.

Landing - fire, steel and earth it threw,
Ah - once again on each man's face color grew.
Leaping Lena was the Rocket then named,
It gave the story of brave men she had claimed.

That night an oath was made which lips did not relate,
"That she be destroyed," that thing which they hate.
And if one would go to that dark hidden mine,
Today - destroyed, a twisted mass of steel they would find.

*Continued...*

## THE MARINES' IMMORTAL ROCK  *(continued)*

They thanked the morning and the light she gave,
Which shone upon brave men rising from their grave.
A familiar body is hit; my heart shed a tear,
No more to smile, a buddy falls near.

To fight forward, falling, dying, but not retreat,
Asking God to guide his weary feet.
Up a straight cliff, down a steep hill,
Ever onward they crawled with a determined will.

Then, after endless suffering, sweat and fight,
The finish of a battle is now in sight.
Old Glory on Mount Suribachi did proudly wave on high,
And every Marine views his flag thru a tear-filled eye.

And when she was rising to her stately place,
Even old Mount Suribachi seemed to bow in grace.
Endless thanks to those who died that we might live,
Lord, pray that they suffer not whilst they give.

Yes, of course, bonds can buy weapons anew,
But God, tell us - what can bring back Marines so true?

## TIRED IS THE SOLDIER
*by: Second Lieutenant Charles G. Monnett, Jr.*
*"G" Company*
*29th Marine Regiment*
*6th Marine Division*
*Written during a rest at Okinowa*

Tired is the soldier—tired of war;
Exhausted from endless days of sleepless nights.
Days in which he thought he could go no more,
Disgusted with the long bloody fights.
Time passed slowly as he saw his buddies go;
One by one they dropped behind.
Many who would no longer know,
The tiredness of the body and mind.

Friends who were old and dear,
Whom he had joked with, talked with and worked.
Would not celebrate the new year.
Because they their duty had not shirked.
Tired is the soldier—he wants to go home,
Home to America, the land of the free.
Never again this world to roam,
Tired is the soldier—very tired is he.

Tired is the soldier—tired of war,
Demoralized by the long nights of screaming shells.
Fatigued from the charges by day,
What was this but the combination of many hells.
How long would it go on this way?
And so were the thoughts of many men,
Who lay in their foxhole.
Wondering what day would bring the end.

## THE LUCKY ONES
*by: Joseph J. Cornish III, Ph.D.*
*Gunnery Sergeant, USMC, VMR 253, Marine Airwing*
*World War II, China*

*Sgt. J.B. Moullette, USMC, expressed this opinion*
*and thus, inspired this poem.*

You were frightened that day,
Shit-scared you might say
'cause the shells had a lesson to teach.
If you thought you were strong
You might find you were wrong,
But you clung to that sand like a leech.

You did what you could,
'cause you knew that you should,
You had an objective to reach.
And not asking why
You gave it a try
'till the enemy lines had been breeched.

But now you're back home
And you feel all alone
In spite of what all of them preach
And now you can see
You'll never get free
No matter which Gods you beseech.

*Continued...*

### THE LUCKY ONES *(continued)*

So each day's the same
It's all just a game,
Life's just a figure of speech
And looking back now
You can clearly see how
The Lucky Ones died on the beach.

## CROSSES OF GREEN
*by: Corporal N. Joseph Aquilano*
*1st Marine Division F.M.F.*
*1942-1946 World War II*

*A tribute to the men of the First Marine Division, F.M.F. who died*
*on the Island of Guadalcanal in the year of 1942 A.D.*

Yes, crosses of green, that's the scene,
They mark the graves of dead Marines.
No crosses of stone over their bones,
Just a box or part of a tree painted green.

Through the darkness of the jungle, and the living hell,
The barking of a machine gun, the flash of the grenade,
He pitches and falls, another grave is made.

We'll make another cross, and paint it green,
To place over the grave of this brave Marine.
He fought for what he knew was right,
His life he lost in the gallant fight.

Have there ever been men greater than these?
Gallant sons, these young Marines.
Men who loved the breath of life,
And love of mother, sweetheart and wife.

Our country is now at stake.
We'll show the world we can give as well as take.
Take up your arms, you men in green,
Show our enemy the fight of the Marines.

*Continued...*

## CROSSES OF GREEN *(continued)*

The Corps and Country will honour you,
You men that have died on the scene.
We'll erect a cross with your name,
A cross for you Marines, painted green.

## THOSE WHO DIED
### (in the First World War)
*by: Corporal N. Joseph Aquilano*
*1st Marine Division F.M.F.*
*1942-1946 World War II*

They fought for peace, for peace they fell,
As deep as "Dante" into hell.
Midst roaring guns and burning gas,
They lost their lives so peace would last.

But as we see the world today,
We know their lives were lost in vain.
For now again the cannons roar,
To destroy more men and make hearts sore.

Oh, Lord, above. Keep us free and pure,
And immune to all war's hellish lure.

## WHITE CROSSES
*by: Corporal N. Joseph Aquilano*
*1st Marine Division F.M.F.*
*1942-1946 World War II*

Four-thousand white crosses in hundreds of rows,
Mark America's dead soldiers.
Peace at end, World at War,
Will we add more to that gallant score?

Mothers were crying,
Sons were dying,
Will America again---
Send help to her friends?

As for myself and thousands I know,
We'll beg America to let her friends go.
America stay free—keep out of that mess,
Or we'll have more crosses for the Lord to bless.

## CAPE GLOUCESTER
*by: Corporal N. Joseph Aquilano*
*1st Marine Division F.M.F.*
*1942-1946 World War II*

The rain fell on their faces,
It blends in with their tears.

And now the land is richer,
Than it has been, in many many years.

For here these lads did battle,
So strong and so brave.

We're all here to honour you,
We who still remain.

And Old Glory waves above you,
To guard your precious gain.

And with each lad that falls here,
The land drinks more than gold.

For the richness of America,
Is in these lads so bold.

And when the tide of battles cease,
And the world restored to peace.

We'll always remember Cape Gloucester,
And the names left off the roster.

# EIGHT GRAVES

*by: Corporal N. Joseph Aquilano*
*1st Marine Division F.M.F.*
*1942-1946 World War II*

*In honor of the first eight men of the 2nd. Bat. 1st Marine Reg.*
*who lost their lives on New Briton. Dec. 1943.*

They've reached the place where they will rest,
Eight brave Marines, who gave their best,
Here they lie, in eight new graves,
In a place far from the land they saved.

Farewell mates, rest in peace,
We'll tell the world of your feat.
Lift high your heads, eight mother's brave,
The country honours the sacrifice you've made.

Eight Sons, Eight Souls, Eight Graves,
Eight Marines, their lives they gave.

## FIDES, NON ARMIS
**(By Faith, Not by Arms)**
*by: Corporal N. Joseph Aquilano*
*1st Marine Division F.M.F.*
*1942-1946 World War II*

Though to death I may walk,
But not with fear.
For God, The Almight,
Is always near.

What greater assurance,
of peace can there be?
Than the words of the "Our Father"
Whispered to me?

Through the darkest hours,
They may come to my life.
With the help of the Virgin,
I'll always find light.

Fall on your knees,
You battled worn men.
Ask for forgiveness,
And peace once again.

What shame, what sorrow,
Befell on man?
They denounce him,
Who created them.

*Continued...*

## FIDES, NON ARMIS *(continued)*
## (By Faith, Not by Arms)

Again he is crucified,
And bled till he died.
By man and his wildness,
And wearied battle cry.

Pray for us Mary,
And the evil we've done.
Help us find peace,
With the Lord, Thy Son.
Amen.

## BALLAD OF AMERICA
*by: Corporal N. Joseph Aquilano*
*1st Marine Division F.M.F.*
*1942-1946 World War II*

We're young and strong,
With will and determination.
We're the boys,
That will defend the nation.

Our mighty ships,
Upon the seas,
To warn all nations,
We'll stay free.
Our air armada grows each day,
Our pilots young to lead the way.

The workers in the shops
Shan't rest,
Till America has the best.
They'll manufacture guns and shells,
Armored tanks and planes as well.

The farmers grow the grain and wheat,
So soldiers' stomachs won't get weak.
Sure we're young,
But we're strong son-o'-guns.

*Continued...*

### BALLAD OF AMERICA  *(continued)*

We'll fight with every ounce of blood,
To preserve the freedom
That we love.
Oh! Stars and stripes
Shining bright,
Be our own guiding light.

Freedom, freedom is your call,
Never, never let it fall.

## THE COME BACK
*by: Corporal N. Joseph Aquilano*
*1st Marine Division F.M.F.*
*1942-1946 World War II*

He talks about the home front,
And how the going's tough.
(Never giving a thought,
to the man living in the rough.)

He says the price of meat's too high,
And beer is too hard to get.
(There are guys out here that pray for rain,
to drink water from the drain.)

Take off the ration on the gas,
I'd like to do more traveling.
(Yeah! and if I had more gas,
my tank would still be rattling.)

I gave metal for the war,
A good five pounds or more.
(What he's given ain't even enough,
For a shell to reach the shore.)

Look at the taxes!!!
And there's more to come.
(Say, mister, would you rather pay them?
or fire this damn gun?)

## "SIX MORE"

*by: Corporal N. Joseph Aquilano*
*1st Marine Division F.M.F.*
*December 30, 1943, World War II*
*First battle of the 2nd battalion*
*1st Marines at Green Beach Island of New Briton*

Almighty God, there are six more
To add to our glorious score.

The night was black, then came the attack,
Six were lost, but the enemy set back.

They've done their job and done it well,
We trust in you to deliver them from hell.

We men below will always remember
That they lost their lives in the month of December.

We'll drink a toast to that score,
And sing them the hymn of their Corps.

### THAT DAY OF INFAMY
*by: Sergeant George W. Henley*
*Fighter Pilot*
*Corsair F4U-1, the Silver Ghost*

On that peaceful Sunday morning,
Of December 7th Nineteen Forty One
Our ships were all at anchor,
When the Japs made their first run.

There was no hint of troubles,
Our defense system was so lax
Their planes came in about 8 a.m.
And began their first attack.

Their attack was so well planned,
Our battleships were all in a row
But because some officers were negligent,
There was no way our ships could know.

The officers said all those fighter planes
Picked up by our radar men.
Were from our carriers out at sea,
Or new B-17 bombers coming in.

They hit the battleship "Arizona's" magazine,
With a bomb weighing seventeen hundred sixty pound.
And in just a few short minutes,
That mighty ship went down.

*Continued...*

**THAT DAY OF INFAMY** *(continued)*

The battleship "Oklahoma"
With four hundred men inside
Was hit by several torpedos
And rolled over on her side.

The "California" and "West Virginia"
Were sank right where they lay.
The "Utah" capsized with her crew
A horrible price we had to pay.

These mighty ships were damaged,
The "Maryland", "Pennsylvania" and "Tennessee"
Then the "Nevada" tried to make a run
But could not reach the sea.

At 8:40 on that fateful morning
Their second wave came in
They destroyed the "Shaw" and "Sotoyama",
Adding insult to their sin.

They had bombed all of our bases,
Left family life in disarray
They laughed and joked as they flew back north
No apology to this day.

The Japanese had made a big mistake
There is just so much that we will take
And all of these ships, except for three,
Were raised from their grave, to keep us free.

*Continued...*

## THAT DAY OF INFAMY *(continued)*

Our Navy was hurt badly and weakened,
But went out searching the sea, far and wide
They destroyed many enemy ships and planes
The Japanese Navy had no place to hide.

It wasn't long until they knew
That they had a big price to pay
For that one day they bombed "Pearl Harbor"
We bombed and strafed them every day.

Island by island that they controlled
Were slowly being taken away
For our people at home, had built many planes
And the carriers to take them on their way.

We fought them on every island
In the air, on land and sea
We lost a lot of men in battle
They all died for you and me.

The United States came up with a plan
They sent Doolittle's B-25s to bomb Japan
It was now quite clear, the Japanese knew
They were paying the price, for our men they slew.

And then at last, on their fateful day
"Big Boy" was placed on the "Enola Gay"
The atomic bomb was dropped, it was the warning they heeded
We had won the war, no apology given, no apology needed.

### BOMBER'S MOON
*by: Sergeant George W. Henley*
*A night fighter, VMF (N) 533*

Out of the mist and black of night
Out of the silver sea
The pale moon rides to the starlit sky
To light the way for me.

Hard in its lee the shadows stream
Over the sleeping world
Camps and tents and roads revealed
Like tiny maps unfurled.

Out of the dark of clouds I come,
Straight as an arrow's flight;
Hurling death at the earths below-
Bright in the mellow light.

Red and gold the wild flames leap,
Fanned by the hand of death.
Leaving naught but charred remains
Kissed by the glowing breath.

High in the sky the bright moon rides
Lighting the way for me
Out of the smoke and into the night
Over the silver sea.

# VALLEY OF MISSING MEN
*by: Sergeant George Henley USMC*
*April 10, 1945*

*Dedicated to all those men who never returned*

I think back to those islands,
Where gloomy shadows crept,
To look at the graves of my comrades,
Where under the crosses, they slept.

The names were for the record,
But some were known only to God,
Some of our buddies were missing,
Lying unmarked 'neath the sod.

All of the beaches were bloody,
All of the way up to the glen,
Where you see those unmarked crosses,
In the valley of missing men.

Into a home creeps a shadow,
When the horror comes back to them,
But peaceful now is that island,
The home of the missing men.

It seems like the world has forgotten,
You say "NO" but it's happened before,
And the crosses will whiten with age,
'Neath the sand that once reeked with gore.

*Continued...*

## VALLEY OF MISSING MEN *(continued)*

The shadow of a family's heart broken,
Of happiness that could have been,
If their loved one could only return,
From the valley of missing men.

## "THE SILVER GHOST, REDEEMED"
*by: Sergeant George W. Henley*
*Fighter Pilot*
*Corsair F4U-1, the Silver Ghost*

I saw this old beat up Corsair,
There at Eniweotok Atoll;
On an island called Engebi,
As I took my daily stroll.

And beneath that cripples Corsair's wing,
A Marine mechanic stood;
I asked if it could fly again;
He said "I'm sure it could.

He said the Corsair had a past,
They placed her here, to rest at last;
But I could see her, now and then,
Flown hard and fast, by gallant men.

He said "with some effort and tender care,
This bird could be flying in the air".
I could see fullment of my dream,
In this old plane, with silver sheen.

He said the plane had served its time,
And now deserved a rest;
But I knew this plane was searching,
For someone to put her to the test.

*Continued...*

**"THE SILVER GHOST, REDEEMED"** *(continued)*

They had stripped away her coat of blue,
Her hull took on a silver hue;
I knew this plane could fly real fast,
I'd found my perfect plane at last.

We both agreed to spend our time,
To clean off all the dirt and grime;
I know she is ready, and wants to fly,
I promised she would as time goes by.

He tuned her engine to the nth degree,
The rest he said, was up to me;
I spent long hours to wax her wings,
And clean up all the little things.

Several older pilots came by to gape,
Some climbed upon her wing;
Then they all remarked the very same,
"This bird is sure a pretty thing".

Some pilots came by asked to take her up,
But they had said she'd never fly;
So I said "No thanks, she is my girl",
And now its time to do or die.

*Continued...*

## "THE SILVER GHOST, REDEEMED" *(continued)*

There was a lot they never knew,
My silver Corsair, once was blue;
She was a gallant bird, and ready to fly,
And with a little urging, so was I.

One shot was fired and her engine started,
And I heard its mighty roar;
She was telling me, she is ready now,
It's the right time for us to soar.

I taxied her over, to the end of the strip,
We started to roll, she's a beautiful ship;
I gave her full throttle, and she picked up speed,
I pulled back on the stick, that's all she did need.

Now we're clear of the strip, and climbing fast,
I now have a new friend, with a glorious past;
I held the throttle forward, to check her on top speed;
I found she has a lot more, than I would ever need.

Then we flew back to Engebi, I took her in to land,
When we finally reached our tie down space;
They all gave the Silver Ghost a hand,
The old Silver Ghost, they once despised;
After just one flight, was idolized.

*Continued...*

## "THE SILVER GHOST, REDEEMED" *(continued)*

The guys at R & R re-installed her guns,
They knew this lady was back making runs;
The Colonel came to me, said "I've something to say,
You and your silver Corsair, will lead the strike today".

The Colonel never knew all the facts,
That this would be my first bombing run;
But with my trust in the "Silver Ghost,"
I knew it would be fun.

When the strike was over, and we went into land,
All the off duty pilots gave us a big hand;
My Corsair flew circles around the Colonel's Hell Cat,
So I kidded the Colonel, "What do you think of that"?

I'll never forget that beautiful plane,
I'm going home, I must say adieu;
And that was the end of the "Silver Ghost",
They gave her a new coat of blue.

Each time I see a Corsair,
With its gull wings flying by;
My thoughts go back to the "Silver Ghost",
And a tear comes to my eye.

*Continued...*

## "THE SILVER GHOST, REDEEMED" *(continued)*

She handled well, and flew so fast,
She finally found her place at last;
Another man had flown her fast and far,
For the last air battle of the war.

The Marines had landed on Okinawa's shore.
So this gal of mine racks up her score;
With a gallant man to set the pace,
The old "Silver Ghost" made him an ace.

Now, each time I see a Corsair flying by,
I see a "Silver Ghost" there in the sky;
She dips her wings as if to say;
"I know your here, for me today".

When I first saw my Corsair friend,
She had flown her last, it seemed;
But with a lot of love, and some hard work,
The Ghost had been redeemed.

I took my wife to a Marine Air Show,
And met a pilot, I used to know;
He spoke of things, we used to do,
Before the Silver Ghost was painted blue.

## SILVER WINGS
*by: Sergeant George W. Henley*

Silver wings and blazing stars
May take you through the night,
But every pilot turns again,
When day is golden-bright.

And every girl who loves a man
Who ventures forth on winds,
Burns tall and flame-tipped candles
And waits till daylight brings.

The sound of footsteps in the hall,
The quick hand on the door,
And love's hours shared together
Just as they were before.

# UNTITLED
*by: Sergeant George W. Henley*

When I was just a little boy,
I knew that times were bad;
But I think of all the friends we knew,
And all the fun we had.

It wasn't easy on my mom,
With brother, sis and I;
For she worked hard to make ends meet,
And somehow we got by.

But I grew up at an early age,
That's what they all will say;
At the age of twelve, I had a job,
And earned a grown mans pay.

I went to school, just like the rest,
And really tried, and did my best;
My feet were tired, from the long walk,
Me ears were closed to useless talk;

I came to study, not to play,
For school was just, one half my day;
While others dreamed of dates and cars,
My thoughts took wings to distant stars.

*Continued...*

### UNTITLED *(continued)*

I dreamed of a time, I knew not when,
I'd take my place with other men;
I'd settle down in a little home,
Perhaps have children of my own.

But then we had the mighty war,
Not like the ones we had before;
The call rang out thru all the land,
Our nation needed every man.

Tho still a lad, just in my teens,
I donned the green, of the Marines;
They trained me well, then sent me west,
And once again, I did my best.

The Island Empire of Japan,
They too, had called up every man;
All wars are hell, I must agree,
But this one did a lot for me.

We met their best, on land and sea,
And each time had a victory,
But did we win, I wonder now,
Can tanks and guns, become a plow.

*Continued...*

## UNTITLED *(continued)*

Can lives once lost, ee'r be reclaimed,
Or are they lost, in victories name;
The men we fought, were human too,
Their skins were just a different hue.

Their blood ran red, just like ours did,
I met this one, he's just a kid;
We talked and somehow understood,
That wars are wrong, they breed no good.

And as his body slowly mends,
The two of us became good friends;
When he was well, we said goodbye,
I am so glad, he didn't die.

For I had shot this thin young man,
With rifle firmly in my hand;
Thank God, my bullet missed its mark,
For I had aimed straight at his heart.

Perhaps, his God, did intercede,
And made me jerk, instead of squeeze;
My trigger finger may have known,
He had a family, like my own.

*Continued...*

## UNTITLED *(continued)*

Now the war has reached its end,
We're running short on lives to spend;
We can plan for peace, and make it work,
If from our duties, we don't shirk.

Our peace came high, the price was paid,
By millions lying in the grave,
They gave their all, that we might be,
The guiding light, with all men free.

A few years pass, we failed these men,
For battles start to flare again;
Another time, another place,
A soldiers dead, a nameless face.

Strong now, our mighty nation stands,
Once more, we leave our native lands;
But this ones worse, its like a sin,
Our leaders will not, let us win.

The fight goes on, and more men die,
Their wives and children, sit and cry;
Back in the states, their patience spent,
The people choose Ike, their President.

*Continued...*

## UNTITLED *(continued)*

Ike wanted peace, he said it loud,
His words rang true, they pleased the crowd;
He knew our nation could not stand,
Unless he offered them his hand.

The war was stopped, this was our last,
We must remember, all wars past;
What have we gained, by taking life,
And burning homes, and causing strife.

The stories told, that in time of need,
Our every prayer, our God will heed;
We prayed for peace in any name,
It wasn't long until it came.

A few more years go slipping by,
The people smile and breathe a sigh;
But peace can't last, there's too much greed,
Another war, more hearts to bleed.

This war is not the popular kind,
And many men they stayed behind;
Some ran away to a foreign land,
They felt they too, must make a stand.

*Continued...*

### UNTITLED *(continued)*

Our nation's rich, but all its wealth,
Cannot protect our nations health;
Our nation's sick, most folks agree,
This war's not right, for you and me.

Another man, another place,
And Nixon's now in Johnson's place;
This war must end, was his decree,
And so it did...no victory.

Now we're at peace, or so they say,
When parents smile, and children play;
Without the thoughts of fears and dread,
That on the morn, they may be dead.

I pray that soon, all wars shall end,
And we shall find some gallant men;
Who love this land, and further more,
Can bring us peace, from shore to shore.

If politicians had to fight,
They would search for peace;
With all their might,
Its just a thought, and it might be;
The answer friend, for you and me...

## "GRANDPA'S WORDS OF WISDOM"
*by: Sergeant George W. Henley*

I remember the words of wisdom
Grandpa Lemmons spoke to me
Our country is now engaged in war
With a land across the sea.

He said "I'm sure you'll be going soon
So listen carefully to my plea
Our men folks have fought in every war
In recorded history".

Those Japanese have attact Pearl Harbor
They destroyed most ships of the line
So when you do meet, you must never retreat
Do your very best and that will be fine.

So if you do meet them, on land, air, or sea
Remember these words, you hear now from me
I listened and remembered, all the words he then said
If not for these words he told me,
There's a good chance I'd be dead.

You can't go to war and win, my boy
With your conscience on your mind
You must strike first, with all your might
And so leave your conscience far behind.

*Continued...*

## "GRANDPA'S WORDS OF WISDOM" *(continued)*

These words he spoke, were oh so true
For the enemy no conscience knew
We hit them hard, air, land, and sea
Then we thanked our God, for victory.

We had won the war, we were released
And I went back to our farm
Where I had put my conscience in a jar
To protect it from all harm.

Grandma was strong, but Grandpa was sick
But he never was one to be bossed
But she sold the farm, when I left home
Now my conscience jar was lost.

Perhaps some day I shall return
And drive out to the farm
To see if they had touched my spot
Or did my conscience harm.

Someday I'm gonna go again
Cause it's not so very far
And I'll ask the new owners of our farm
To help me find my conscience jar.

## CONSCIENCE LOST
*by: Sergeant George W. Henley*

When I was just a young lad
This country went to war
I couldn't take my conscience along
So I placed it in a jar.

I took that old fruit jar
And buried it on our farm
I buried it a way down deep
To protect if from all harm.

Then off I went to fight a war
No conscience on my mind
For it was in that fruit jar
That I'd left so far behind.

When I came back after the war
I found to my alarm
I couldn't get my conscience back
The folks had sold the farm.

While driving past the farm one day
In my old beat up car
I saw the owners standing o'er
The burial spot of my jar.

*Continued...*

## CONSCIENCE LOST *(continued)*

I walked right out to where they stood
Said I'd once owned this land
And I'd like to get my conscience back
If they would lend a hand.

We dug awhile, I heard a yell
And I looked over thar
That old farmers wife was grinnen
As she held my conscience jar.

I took that jar and grinned right back
And said "I thank you ma'am"
She said "Lookin at that fruit jar boy"
Your conscience must be dammed.

I put that fruit jar in my car
And drove right straight to town
And every time I turned a curve
That fruit jar rolled around.

I saw a pretty little girl
And got her in my car
And every time I made a pass
I thought about that jar.

*Continued...*

## CONSCIENCE LOST *(continued)*

I drove my car out to the bridge
Threw that jar in the crick
I sure don't want that thing around
It makes my love life sick.

And now that jar floats down the stream
Controlled by time and tide
If you see it floating down your way
You better run and hide.

Some day some fool will come along
And find it on the shore
Then he will have my conscience
To live with evermore.

## A LOST COMRADE
*by: Sergeant George W. Henley*

The muffled drum's sad roll has beat,
The soliders last tattoo;
The echo taps, from far away,
Has bid this warrior, a sad adieu.

No more must he ever worry,
About finally facing the foe;
His battles are all left behind him,
He's relieved of all worries and woes.

This warrior now has found his peace,
He will hear no more alarms;
For he's found his final resting place,
Where there is no call to arms.

I pray his glory is not forgot,
When fame her record keeps;
I pray you will care for this hallowed spot,
Where my valiant comrade sleeps.

## ODE TO A MECHANIC
*by: Sergeant George W. Henley*

Under the silver Corsair's wing,
The Marine mechanic stands;
His brow is wet with grease and sweat,
His face a healthy tan.

He toils from dawn to setting sun,
This lonely, tired Gyrene;
He has no rate, and how he hates,
The Japs he's never seen.

When bullets fly from east to west,
To strike his Corsair's wing;
With tool in hand, he takes a stand,
To fix the dad-blamed thing.

He heats his gums from morn to night,
This lowely son of toil;
Just mention Spam or Uncle Sam,
And you'll have a battle royal.

Each rising sun he'd like to take,
And rend him limb to limb;
Then pack his grip, for a stateside trip,
Even if he has to swim.

## THE BATTLE OF SLIPPERY RIDGE
*by: Michael E. Filanowski*
*Third U.S. Marine Raider Battalion*
*1943*

Oh! How can I ever forget
That fateful night in fourty-four.
An event I think of with regret,
An event I still abhor.

The memories of a time long past
Still linger in my mind.
Thoughts that seem to last and last,
Thoughts I cannot leave behind.

The memories of that night are fresh
As if it happened yesterday.
The happenings that would soon enmesh
On that isle so far away.

It is a tale of woe and anguish,
A tale of rueing and hate.
For I do not wish to languish
In this story I will relate.

Harken to me, my brothers
For I'm no longer a prancing stallion.
This message is for others
As well as the third battalion.

*Continued...*

## THE BATTLE OF SLIPPERY RIDGE *(continued)*

It started out so pleasant
With a breakfast of Spam and eggs,
(Now you know that wasn't pheasant)
And coffee with all its dregs.

The noon meal consisted of eggs and Spam
And lemonade so sour.
It wasn't good, but who gave a damn.
You downed it, and didn't cower.

For the evening meal the word went out
That fresh meat would be served.
The men began to sing and shout
And became completely unnerved.

We washed and showered the best we could
In preparation of our feast.
With proper decorum, as a raider should,
Abstain from acting the beast.

The music sounded the chow call.
We rushed to the company street,
And proceeded to the mess hall
To partake in our gourmet treat.

*Continued...*

## THE BATTLE OF SLIPPERY RIDGE *(continued)*

As I approached the table
With knife and spoon and fork,
Lo and behold without fable
Was a roast of Australian pork.

The repast was delicious,
But no one remotely knew,
That beside of being nutritious,
Little worms within it grew.

We gorged ourselves to the utmost,
The burps they did resound.
Whoever would think a pork roast
Would bring elation so profound.

As I retreated to my tent
And laid upon my sack,
I soon began a gaseous vent,
Not from the front, but from the back.

I laid beneath my mosquito net
And began to feeling drowsy.
With pleasant thoughts of stateside, yet
I started feeling lousy.

*Continued...*

## THE BATTLE OF SLIPPERY RIDGE *(continued)*

I was soon overtaken by blessed sleep
And dreamed of good things to come,
Of cans of beer in ice so deep,
And the pretty girls back home.

Then all of a sudden I felt a jolt
And suddenly to my behoovement,
From my sack I sprang just like a bolt
For I sensed a bowel movement.

I tried to dress with the utmost speed
And pull boondockers on my feet.
The obstacles before me I did not heed
As I ran to the company street.

I sped around the rows of tents,
The night was moonless and dark.
And let me assure you, my fellow gents,
I wasn't playing the lark.

I raced across the coconut log bridge
That spanned the drainage ditch,
And headed for the head on the ridge
So far without a hitch.

*Continued...*

## THE BATTLE OF SLIPPERY RIDGE  *(continued)*

As I bolted up the darkened path
I doubled up with pain.
It ached and pained like no fury hath
Then I knew it was in vain.

I knew I had to get fast relief,
So beside the path I did squat.
I shouted, "Fire in the hole!" and beyond belief
It came out like a shot.

I thought I was the only lad,
No one could have predicted.
I soon found out that others had
Likewise been afflicted.

For as I squatted beside the trail,
Others crossed the bridge.
Some succeeded and some did fail
To make it to the ridge.

First there were two, then three, then four,
That came across that bridge.
Then five and six, then a couple of score,
All racing for the ridge.

*Continued...*

## THE BATTLE OF SLIPPERY RIDGE  *(continued)*

One young lad, he passed me by
Then came to a screeching halt.
He bowed his head and began to cry
As if he were at fault.

He slowly lifted the leg of his pants
And gently began to shake it.
I surmised it was a pretty good chance
That he clearly did not make it.

Slowly did he turn around
And headed from whence he came.
His disgust was clearly so profound
And his head was bowed in shame.

It took some time to figure out,
As my mind did delve upon,
As to the cause of this fiendish rout
And what the hell was going on.

And so it went on through the night,
A thousand men in trouble.
It lasted past the morning's light,
By luck it wasn't double.

*Continued...*

## THE BATTLE OF SLIPPERY RIDGE *(continued)*

Need I say no breakfast was served,
The cooks were unable to work.
For they just got what they well deserved
By eating their own roast pork.

We all lined up at sick bay,
The corpsmen were allerted.
Medication soon was on its way,
And a panic was averted.

The corpsmen and doctors, God bless their souls,
Acted anything but euphoric.
Why, by far they surpassed their goals
In dispensing of Paragoric.

Their work was made exceedingly hard,
No one could have depicted.
They did their job without regard,
For they also were afflicted.

Things soon began to simmer down,
We began to feeling hearty.
Upon command and without frown
We formed a working party.

*Continued...*

## THE BATTLE OF SLIPPERY RIDGE *(continued)*

We began to advance upon the knoll
Armed with a trenching tool.
Excavating a little fox hole
For each and every stool.

As we skirmished up the hillside,
How greatly we were surprised.
Our amazement we could hardly hide
How well it was fertilized.

We finally made it to the crest,
The victory we had won.
We sat down for a needed rest
And boasted of a job well done.

The air was full of a putrid smell,
And as you might surely guess,
The heartiest man it did repell,
For the ridge was a slippery mess.

We slowly decended from the ridge.
Our satisfaction was immense
As we crossed the coconut log bridge
And headed for our tents.

*Continued...*

## THE BATTLE OF SLIPPERY RIDGE *(continued)*

In order to regain our strength
A day of rest was granted,
And try to dream sweet dreams at length
That this scourge of ours supplanted.

For this gallant and courageous act
The entire third battalion
As a matter of record and of fact
Received a bronze medallion.

How lucky we were no Japs were about
For I fear with a shudder and frown,
Had they attacked with their banzai shout
They'd have caught us with our pants down.

The lesson I've learned from this sad tale
Is from pork you should abstain.
If you want to be healthy, hearty and hale,
You've got nothing to lose, but gain.

Let no one be mistaken,
My goal is a centenarian.
For pork I've clearly foresaken
And I'm a die-hard vegetarian.

*Continued...*

## THE BATTLE OF SLIPPERY RIDGE *(continued)*

Now I end this tale of woe
That I tried to unabridge,
And narrate to all, both friend and foe,
THE BATTLE OF SLIPPERY RIDGE.

P.S. Those of you who doubt this tale
That I tried to truly tell,
I tried by best, so without fail
You can all go straight to ....
....the next Raider reunion, and have a drink on me.

## FIRST MARINE DIVISION
*by: Corporal John J. McLeod*
*7th Marines, First Marines Division*
*The Battle of the Invasion of Okinawa, 1945*

*(Tune of the "Marine's Hymn")*

From the shores of Okinawa
To the city of Tokyo
The First Marine Division
Is always on the go
We're the first to make a beachhead
And the last to ever leave
We are always in there fighting
Those no good Japanese.

We have fought in the Pacific
The first was Guadalcanal
We have a punch that's terrific
And we always give them hell
Oh, the Japs they are everywhere
Even under the ground, it seems
And the ones that always keep them there
Are the First Division Marines

## OKINAWA CONVOY
*by: Corporal John J. McLeod*
*7th Marines, First Marines Division*
*The Battle of the Invasion of Okinawa, 1945*

*(Tune of "Chattanooga Choo Choo")*

Pardon me boy, this is the Okinawa Convoy
Ship 199, Will reach our objective on time
I can afford to board the Okinawa Convoy
Uncle Sam pays my fare.
Because there's nippies over there.
You leave the Russell Island Pier
About a quarter to four, check up on your gear
Because you're going to war
Dinner in the diner, could be so much finer
But what the hell, this is not a liner.
When you hear planes winging over head,
You hurry below deck but they're ours instead.
You get a lot of briefing, also lots of sleeping
Okinawa Shima lies dead ahead.
There's going to be, a bunch of nippies on the mountains,
Mortors will fall and they will try for us all
But they're going to die for the glory of the setting sun,
Oh, Okinawa Shima our work here is done.

**Korea: Rifleman, winter dress**
*Artwork by Andy Carroll*
*from Elite Series 2: The US Marine Corps Since 1945*
© *Osprey Publishing*

# KOREAN WAR

## (1950 - 1953)

| | |
|---|---|
| Total service members | 5,720,000 |
| Battle deaths | 33,686 |
| Other deaths in service (theater) | 2,830 |
| Other deaths in service (nontheater) | 17,730 |
| Nonmortal woundings | 103,284 |
| Living veterans (69)[1] | 2,976,446 |

1. Median ages.

*Source: Department of Defense and Veterans Administration, Sept. 30, 2001.*

## US MARINES
*by: Sergeant A. J. Kozlowski, Jr.*
*USMC (1204578)*
*Korea 1952*

There goes a *United States Marine*
A real bold man, strong and clean
He has fought for life and death
*Marines* won't give up on that you can bet

Some of them are big or small in size
But their fighting tactics are most wise
Yes, they are men of different race and creed
Always sticking together when in the need

In case we shall fall into a tragic war
The fighting *US Marines* will beat them as before
If the enemy tries to make us the loss
We'll just show them that *Marines* are boss

They will fight for American's every right
Should it be during the day or night
On these, *US Marines* all can depend
The boys who will fight from the start to the end!

## THE DEBT THAT WAS PAID
*by: Corporal A. G. (Robbie) Robinson, USMC*
*Radioman, MTACS-2 One of the many*
*voices of "Devastate Baker"*

*Submitted by: Robert M. Todd*

*This poem was written shortly before Cpl. Robinson was*
*listed "Missing in Action" in defense of HAGARU perimeter,*
*28-29 November 1950*


A bunch of Marines were sweating it out
in the South Korean hills.
The kid that handled the BAR,
was taking Atabrine pills.

While back of the kid, in the black of night,
sat a solemn group of men.
Pondering in their next move only,
wondering where and when.

When out of the night, all muddy and wet,
into the view of them all.
There stumbled a private packing a buddy
almost ready to fall.

They stared with wonder and awe,
at the pitiful sight they saw
All were hoping the man out there
would make it without a flaw.

*Continued...*

## THE DEBT THAT WAS PAID *(continued)*

When all at once the sky lit up
with the help of an enemy flare.
And the sharp report of machinegun fire
put a smell of death in the air.

But soon the firing ended
and the men they looked around,
But their comrade hadn't made it,
He'd fell dead upon the ground.

His body was cut to ribbons,
and they turned from the sight out there.
And it seemed that the world paid homage
as they knelt in silent prayer.

So this was the way it was meant to be,
for this the reds would pay
There might be others who would retreat,
but the Marines were here to stay.

Soon they were given a mission,
so they cinched their belts up tight,
And started down the sloppy trail
to give the reds a fight.

They vowed a lot of enemy deaths
would take place with their aid,
A lot of stinking reds
would be green of Chinese Jade.

*Continued...*

# THE DEBT THAT WAS PAID *(continued)*

They now were told their mission,
a communist machinegun nest,
To wipe this out before the dawn,
they had to do their best.

Through a rice paddy, crawling for now,
for they know the enemy is near.
Before too long a time had passed,
the lead-man gave a cheer.

Just to the right and a little above,
sat their target for tonight,
There's just four commies sitting there,
thinking things were right.

Now old Big Mike, he spoke up first,
for this was a one-man job,
He'd lost his younger brother today
and this would pay for Bob.

The night was awful quiet
and he crept toward his goal,
It looked like someone with him,
Bob's worn and weary soul.

He held the Browning lightly
for the job was all his now,
He inched up ever closer
with warm sweat on his brow.

*Continued...*

## THE DEBT THAT WAS PAID *(continued)*

Now, he thought, was the time to do it,
now is the time for this.
This was to him all alone,
Lord what a beautiful dish.

And then when he pulled the trigger,
what a glorious sound it made
Now Mike could rest and live in peace,
Bob's debt had just been paid.

Yes, four Reds would have it quiet today
in the South Korean hills,
Where the kid that handles the BAR,
is taking Atabrine pills.

# 4TH BATT MIKE BTRY
*by: Corporal Robert J. Hurley*
*Battery Recorder with Mike Battery*
*4th Battalion, 11th Marines,*
*1st Marine Division, Korea 1951*

*Submitted by: Salvatore Spinicchia*

I record, 4th battalion, Mike Battery,
With 11th Marines Artillery.
And the competition gets real keen,
In the 4th battalion, 11th Marines.

For its C.S.M.O. when things are hot,
And the battery moves to another spot.
You dig em in and set em up,
And grab some coffee in your canteen cup.

At first the guns would keep you awake,
But you learn to sleep in a 10 minute break.
And you learn to move on the double quick,
When the missions are coming fast and thick.

We have to support the infantry,
To give em fire where it ought to be.
Our boys move up, the battle's won,
The enemy's bleedin and on the run.

Then its C.S.M.O. and the dust is dense,
And the Captain's gone to reconnaissance.
He drives up the road and finds a field,
And we set up our guns with the shamrock shield.

*Continued...*

## 4TH BATT. MIKE BTRY *(continued)*

The gunners curse the cannonars,
Who swallow their anger and hold their tears.
They do their job and don't complain,
As they ram em home and sweat and strain.

Now the men in the batt. who have gone before,
Just march right up to the "golden door".
And they know St. Peter will open the gate,
Or they'll call to their friends for a Battery 8.

They join the angels artillery,
With men from old Mike Battery.
Using thunder for powder n' lightning for shells,
They give the devil plenty of hell.

Our guns will roar till the shooting's done,
And the smoke has cleared and the war is won.
Then the old 4th Battalion, 11th Marines,
Will return to the states and training routine.

# WHAT A MARINE THINKS
*by: Private First Class Elmer J. Smith*
*1st Marine Division*
*Korea 1951*

I am a Marine of only nineteen
Who fights a battle across the sea,
It's not just the honor so bright,
It's for your Mom and Pop,
To be able to sleep at night.

This is the reason we are here today,
Because so many people forgot to pray.
I know it seems just like a game,
But we still fight in the mud and rain.

So you look up to heaven, which is so bright,
And pray that God may pass you through the night.
Yes, war is a funny thing, you say to yourself.
It's mostly thinking of your Mom and Pop
Than it is thinking of yourself.

You wait for the day when you hear them say,
That's my son who's been away.
Yes, it's those two people you are fighting for,
Because they are the ones you adore.

You ask me if this thing war is right,
You may sit in a foxhole all during the night
That brings chills to your body,
And thoughts of fright.

*Continued...*

## WHAT A MARINE THINKS *(continued)*

I am a Marine and best outfit I know,
The men are proud of their fame and foe.
I know my Mom and Pop think proudly of me,
For I am across the wide open sea.

This is why I'm proud to serve,
Because my Mom and Pop gave me my nerve.
Yes, this is what a Marine thinks,
As he sits in a foxhole that slowly sinks.
Yes, that's what this Marine thinks.

## ODE TO KOREA
*by: Sergeant Robert Wirth, Sr.*
*"C" Company*
*1st Engineer Battalion*
*1st Marine Division*

This intrepid lad,
Went overseas-
To save that land,
From the Red Chinese-

He's fought thru, the winters' blizzards,
And under the hot old sun-
So he may return home again,
When his job is done-

His only thoughts, no matter where,
Still remain the same-
About the states, his home,
Or maybe a special dame-

The foxholes, that he digs,
May very well, be his grave-
But he knows, the freedom he fights for,
Is what he has to save-

On the move all the time,
With hardly time to eat-
To help repel the enemy,
From which, there is no retreat-

*Continued...*

## ODE TO KOREA *(continued)*

He asks for no glory,
Nor does he want the fame-
He knows he has a job to do,
So he digs right in again-

Things don't always, go the way,
That plans are made up for-
But lives are lost, along with friends,
So he must try and even up the score-

So he's not a big movie hero,
But just another guy-
They're all in this together,
Though clouds may darken the sky-

Rice paddies, are his home,
Since first, he came to this land-
He will fight, to save his life,
No matter what the demands-

He fights his way, over the mountains,
And thru the paddies, deep with rain-
He sees his comrades, fall beside him,
Never to rise again-

When peace again, conquers all,
And to the states, returns this native son-
In his heart, a happy thought,
About a job well done-

*Continued...*

## ODE TO KOREA  *(continued)*

So goes the sad grim story,
Of a man, who has lived thru hell-
To protect all his loved ones,
From the enemy, he knew so well-

The globe and anchor, is his symbol,
It stands for the fighting, he's seen-
No other can claim this title,
Except a United States Marine-

## KOREA

*by: Sergeant Robert Wirth, Sr.*
*"C" Company*
*1st Engineer Battalion, 1st Marine Division*

In the deep South Pacific Paradise,
Lies a spot, that could pass for hell-
It's name is rather simple,
It's Korea, bet you know it well-

It consists entirely of mountains,
Mostly the big ones you see-
If by chance, you ever go there,
With me, you will agree-

There's people there, 20 million or so,
That don't know right from wrong-
They have somewhat of a country loyality,
But will change it, for a song-

"Hava no" and "washie washie,"
Are their two main words of speech-
And if to one, you offer something,
The others cling to you, like a leech-

I'd like to sum up my theory,
On what the name Korea can mean-
After you've read it over,
Good sense, My theory may seem-

*Continued...*

## KOREA *(continued)*

K- Stands for the kruddy place that it is,
O- Is the oriental touch-
R- Is religion, it has none,
E- Is education, it hasn't much-

A- the last of the letters,
Means simply one thing more-
And this is awful, and Korea is that,
Only more so, but here we'll close the door-

Too many facts about this place,
Can turn even the strong stomach-
So you can probably, tell by now,
This place isn't worth a lick-

## LINE KANSAS 1951
*by: Robert de Castro*
*Korea 1950-52*
*11th Marines, 1st Division*

We broke the Morning Calm
With thunder towed with six-bys.
With shrieking steel and flame hurled through soundless skies;
With thunder offending ears and earth and enemy;
We brought spring to twice won, twice wounded slopes.

No larks, whose cries might have been
"Scarce heard by guns below" accompanied our overture.
No, not for our war.

Were you in the "Big One"?
They issued us your weapons and your gear,
But not your kind of victory.
No final curtain rang down on our theater;
No applause and 'exeunt omnes'.

If we could return and endure for you
The mud of Cape Gloucester,
The madness of Peleliu,
The malaria of Guadalcanal,
Would you trade us your bright yellow ribbon
For our cold blue?

*Continued...*

## LINE KANSAS 1951 *(continued)*

No. And rightly so.
For we fought not for parades and handshakes
But, like you, because we were there, and it was our time.
And yes, like you we fought for Corps and especially for each other.

We forged a bond- that's the thing.
And how we did it
I remember every spring.

## ONCE UPON A LIFETIME
*by: C. I. Greenwood*
*Gunnery Sergeant USMC Ret.*

It began at Parris Island,
many years ago,
I wanted to do my part
to travel to and fro.

I signed up for the best I thought
the Corps was the place for me,
Soon I'd be a hero
some place across the sea.

But first I did some duty
as guard and brig boss too,
This ain't the way I planned it
but who the hell could I sue?

It wasn't too much later when
from D.C. the word came down,
Get your seabag packed my lad,
you're gonna leave this town.

There's a place they call Korea
been attacked by this Commie lot,
Their homes have been burned,
and their women and children shot.

*Continued...*

## ONCE UPON A LIFETIME *(continued)*

The North invaded South Korea
and with this Commie crew
it wouldn't take them long
before they'd be in a stew.

MacArthur said I'll need Marines
'Cause landings they do so well,
They're proud of their work, they never quit,
they'd sooner go to Hell.

They came from posts & stations
from over this whole land,
Each would do his part
and lend a helping hand.

Camp Pendleton was where we trained
for a war it seemed like then,
Who would have ever thought
we weren't supposed to win?

The Commies, we were told
are worse than Attilla the Hun.
We're going there to fight
And this one might be fun.

*Continued...*

## ONCE UPON A LIFETIME *(continued)*

So train we did and quickly too
the South can't hold forever!
The Commies have too many men,
already they've broke through.

When they thought that we were ready,
and we gave all we could give
They sailed us on the ocean and
called us FIRST MAR DIV.

It's 5 P.M., daylight gone
and surely we are lost
what did you say's the name of this place
did some call it In-chon?

I must admit that I was scared
'cause seawalls I'd never seen.
But I only had to scale that wall
to earn the name Marine.

Well scale it we did and a beachhead we had
and the enemy knew at a glance
they weren't fighting women and kids.
We came to kick their pants!

Inchon was ours, YongDungPo too
and Seoul fell quick like a song,
rest for a day for tomorrow we sail and land,
at a place called Wonsan.

*Continued...*

## ONCE UPON A LIFETIME *(continued)*

Wonsan we took but we're not done yet
don't they know when enough's enough?
Wait till you see what's coming up next
if you think the last few were tough.

Northward we climbed, the mountains were ice
and most of our bodies were frozen.
Cheer up lads, we're finally here
Welcome to the Frozen Chosin!

The enemy we drove to the banks of Yalu
and we took a day of rest.
We were veterans now
and had surely passed the test.

Now if you believe in Murphy's law
where the worst can happen will,
look out yonder at the Chinese hordes
a comin' o'er the hill.

We've fought for days and fought for nights,
sleep is a thing of the past.
It's 40 below and I want to know
how long does this damned thing last?

I'm no longer tired, the fear is gone
I feel the pain no more.
My comrades are so scattered about.
Will someone please tell me the score.

*Continued...*

### ONCE UPON A LIFETIME *(continued)*

It seems like we killed them once
and maybe once again.
But they just keep on comin' and
our numbers are getting thin.

Then Murphy's law showed up again.
Wouldn't you know it would?
Truman fired MacArthur—
he said he thought he should.

We fought like hell to get us here
Pray now what do we do?
About face, Truman said,
you're advancing to the rear.

So retreat we did against our will
Our Commander-in-Chief had spoken.
Write them off the books he said,
their ranks have been so broken.

Did you ever see a six-by truck
with a hundred bodies aboard?
A ghastly sight, all frozen stiff
gone to meet their Lord.

But look around, some's still here
there's Bill, there's Fletch and Luke.
Eyes straight ahead, don't look back
those trucks will make you puke.

*Continued...*

## ONCE UPON A LIFETIME *(continued)*

There's Emil C. and also Ski,
and damn it, I'm here too.
If they think we're quitting now
Have I got news for you.

We're going down that Hill
My comrades at my side.
Get off your butt and move it out
We've got to make the tide.

We fought a dozen nights and days
to come from Hag-A-Ru.
Killing those damned Commies
and fight the weather too.

Have you ever seen a battleship
or heard its awesome roar?
There sits the ship Missouri
off that Hag-A-Ru shore.

Her cannons spoke so deadly sweet,
and later we'd buy the beer
For all those lovely shells she lobbed
to cover up our rear.

Then we all broke up I guess
and went our separate way.
I don't know where they are right now,
but I wonder day to day.

*Continued...*

## ONCE UPON A LIFETIME *(continued)*

I stayed on myself,
Like Buff and Lucas too.
I recruited men and drilled some troops
To finish out my tour.

Then one quick trip to Vietnman
across the briny sea.
I crossed the ocean one more time
and that ended it for me.

It's been twenty years or more
give or take a few.
They say that I'm retired now
but are we ever through?

Did I forget to mention
along the way a wife,
two daughters and two sons
that added to my life?

I'm older now, and solider no more,
but still I do my bit.
I raise my flag and I vote
but mostly I just sit.

I remember well that rainy day,
that Inchon Wall, so far away.
We fought for issues now long dead
"police action" I think they said.

*Continued...*

## ONCE UPON A LIFETIME *(continued)*

But I'd do it over all again
a thousand times or more.
If I could keep those Commies
from being on our shore.

**Note:** This poem is from Mr. Greenwood's book entitled "Once Upon a Lifetime". If you would like to receive a copy of his book please send $6.50 (includes P&H) to:

TOMAHAWK PUBLISHING
159 Gabriel Road
Springfield, Ill. 62702

All proceeds are used for the upkeep of the "ILLINOIS KOREAN WAR MEMORIAL"

# CHOSIN ELEGY
*by: Sergeant Graydon A. Landahl*
*December 2, 2000*

*In Memoriam of the 50th Anniversary of the epic battle*
*of the "Chosen Reservoir"*

We haunt the hills and valleys,
The frozen draws, we wail in
Darkness of the snowblown nights,

We are the voices of the souls returned
To God in battle,
We are the voices forever frozen in time,

We neither sleep nor laugh, nor are there tears shed here,
There is no rank or hierarchy here,
We are all one, the voices of the Chosin dead,

We cannot leave the battlefields on which we gave our all,

Through all eternity your memories will host our voices clear,
We are the framework of the fraternity of honor,
The Chosin Few.

We are suspended in our own dimension,
We have not aged, as you, though fifty years have passed,

*Continued...*

## CHOSIN ELEGY *(continued)*

We deeply felt the grief our families could not shake,
When we did not return,
The shock and sadness of our buddies,
when we were killed next to them,
Or when they learned at morning's light the deadly toll of friends
No more to be seen in life—we felt and remembered,

We voices understand how difficult these memories are
That you have carried all these years,

They are precious remembrances,
They cannot be bought or sold at any price.

We voices are forever young, and in our
Youthful exuberance we urge you
Not to forget that we died for a way of
Life, freedom, dignity, love of others, for you.

We cannot leave these frozen battlefields
Though all our bones be re-interred,
You alone can honor our place, and
Your place in history, through
Fellowship and love,

Each one of you has an honored place, one
Is not above another, each gave
According to what they were called
Upon to give, we gave our all,
Our lives.

*Continued...*

## CHOSIN ELEGY *(continued)*

The "voices of the Chosin" are here with
You remembering the immortal spirit
That connects us still, and always will,

We are in your hearts and minds,
We are in your stories, the hills around
Yudam-ni, the firefights, Toktong Pass,
The seesaw battles of East hill,
The Hagaru perimeter, the road
Back to Koto-ri, one long firefight,
Day and night, every man a fighting machine,
Selfless devotion to each other.
Heroism beyond belief, unquestioned bravery,
Undaunting courage; untold stories by the
Thousands; we voices were there.

Be silent, you can hear our voices in
The winter winds of Chosin, we speak
To each of you as brothers, the
Sacrifice we made is branded in your
Flesh, and in your soul.

We Chosin voices grieve alone for those
Who have forgotten the humility of
Brotherhood, born in blood and hardship.

We ask that you and we be one in victory,
In remembrance of our shared sacrifice.
This is the elegy of the Chosin voices.

**Vietnam, 1967–70: Rifleman**
*Artwork by Andy Carroll*
*from Elite Series 2: The US Marine Corps Since 1945*
*© Osprey Publishing*

# VIETNAM WAR

## (1964 - 1975)

| Total service members | 9,200,000 |
|---|---|
| Deployed to Southeast Asia | 3,100,000 |
| Battle deaths | 47,410 |
| Other deaths in service (theater) | 10,788 |
| Other deaths in service (nontheater) | 32,000 |
| Nonmortal woundings | 153,303 |
| Living veterans (55)[1] | 7,495,029 |

1. Median ages.

*Source: Department of Defense and Veterans Administration, Sept. 30, 2001.*

### FIRE MISSION
*by: Lance Corporal Michael P. Prikril*
*Dang Ha, Vietnam*
*May 27, 1969*

Fire Mission, the call comes down
I take the grid and pass it round.
It goes to the guns, they lock and load
The grid is cleared, our friendlies told.
"Shouts out" from the cannons stout.

It flies through the air like a bird in flight.
It hits its target to alls delight.
The word "splash" from the observer's mouth
No more will those V.C. shout,
No more will they walk about.

I sit and wonder what I have done.
I took a life which has just begun.
Then I think thoughts that night
Of how their loved ones are alone tonight.
How long will they continue this fight.

I do not think on the subject long.
Rockets are coming, the night is long.
I pray to the Lord while out of sight
Let me see one more night.
Oh God, be with me tonight.

*Continued...*

**FIRE MISSION**  *(continued)*

I wonder if the man on the other gun
Is thinking what he has done.
We only do what must be done
We fight a war which both want won.
"Fire Mission," and I pass it to the gun.

## LETTER FROM HOME
*by: Lance Corporal Michael P. Prikril*
*Dang Ha, Vietnam*
*June 10, 1969*

A letter from home,
What a grand old sight
A gleam in my eye
As I hold it tight.

A picture from the family,
I know they care
I can see in their face
They know why I'm here.

A tear on the paper,
I don't snicker or sneer
I know it's hard for them
While I'm over here.

Yes, that letter from home
Is a grand old sight
I don't care what it says
As long as they write.

# PRAYER TO THE LORD
*by: Lance Corporal Michael P. Prikril*
*Dang Ha, Vietnam*
*June 10, 1969*

A buddy is gone
God rest his soul
His loved ones wait
On their warrior's faith

He gave his life
So others could be free
He never asked the question
Why was it me

Yet people at home
Sing and smoke pot
They never gave thought
To this once warm heart

They talk of peace
And a world to be
But don't they know
You must fight to stay free

When I get home
I will not make light
Of a man who died
To keep an eternal light

So sing if you may
Of a world to be
But pray the Lord
It's not in front of me

## THINGS HAVE CHANGED
*by: Lance Corporal Michael P. Prikril*
*Dang Ha, Vietnam*
*June 10, 1969*

As I sit and listen
To the music as it plays
It brings back thoughts
Of far better days

It makes me remember
The kid on the block
Not giving a damn
About things like jungle rot

Times have changed
And so has he
He's become a man
This, anyone can see

No longer does he walk with a girl
Arm around her waist
It is now rifle he holds
as he steps out the pace

Yes, things have changed
For that kid on the block
He now gives a damn
Even about jungle rot

## THE HOOCH
*by: Lance Corporal Michael P. Prikril*
*Dang Ha, Vietnam*
*June 10, 1969*

We sit in a circle
At the end of each day
It sure was a hot one
That's what we always say

We scrounge up some soda
Hoping it's cold
Then talk of our past
The same story told

Of Mom and of Sis
Standing on the porch
And always of girlfriends
Carrying the torch

This is our joy
Simple it may be
If you can't understand it
It's because you're not we

# ANOTHER DAY

*by: Lance Corporal Michael P. Prikril*
*Dang Ha, Vietnam*
*June 22, 1969*

The day is done
And so am I
I climbed a mile
Into the sky

All day long
I walked and cursed
All day long
My throat did thirst

But now I can rest
My rifle and I
I lie myself down
And watch the night sky

The stars as they shine
With a brilliance so bright
Reminds me of home
And a soft warm light

But the thought soon fades
As the sun comes up
I saddle my gear
And once more am up

Another day
In this land of woe
Another day
To fight the foe

## REFLECTION

*by: Lance Corporal Michael P. Prikril*
*Dang Ha, Vietnam*
*June 24, 1969*

As a boy
I used to play war
Now as a man
I do it once more

I fired my toy
And shot you dead
But now it's for real
As I hang my head

I stormed the beaches
In the corner lot
I do it once more
My stomach a knot

A game to me
It is no more
I hope my children
Never see war

## THE UNSPOKEN
*by: Lance Corporal Michael P. Prikril*
*July 1969*

Denny in the corner
Thinking of his girl at home
Wondering next
Where he will roam

Then there's Jim
Who plays with drums
We call him the weird one
Might say he's just a bum

Can't forget Dave
Who's next in line
Talk of his tractor
Is his only wine

And good ole Worm
The runt in the group
Give him a set of wheels
And he'll fly the coop

Of course there's Gary
Lying in his rack
Just counting the days
Till he gets back

*Continued...*

## THE UNSPOKEN *(continued)*

Granville comes next
Always with something on his chest
But he's a funny guy
Though none of us can figure why

Kid is here
Guzzling his beer
A day hasn't gone by
That he was dry

So this is my hooch
Which we call home
All knowing of the other
The thoughts he does not utter

## QUESTIONS
*by: Lance Corporal Michael P. Prikril*

What can I say
To the people at home
What do I tell em
When I write home

Not of the rockets
We took last night
It will only make them
Shiver with fright

It's harder on them
It seems to me
They wonder about
All that could be

But that is war
So I am told
It effects everyone
No matter how old

So I'll write home
As much as I can
To ease their thoughts
Concerning this land.

## TIME TO REMEMBER
*by: Lance Corporal Michael P. Prikril*

To drink a cold soda,
To have a cold beer
This is what I'll long for
This coming year.

The guys in the bar,
The girl up the block
These will I miss
As I watch the clock.

A clean white sheet
A meal that is hot
What more can I ask for
I can think of not.

These are simple things,
But they're important to me.
And chances are good
That others will agree.

A year gone to waste,
That it is not
It's a time to remember
All that we've got.

They don't seem like much
Till they're taken away,
I'll never appreciate more
The things I miss today.

## ODE TO A MODERN-DAY KNIGHT
*by: John T. Maxwell III*

What does every little boy want?
A Hero for a Dad!
And I am the luckiest boy alive,
For that is what I had!

My Dad was a knight in shining armor,
Though painted in drab green,
His steed was a helicopter,
For my Dad was a Marine!

He rescued soldiers in distress
Braving bullets dragon-hot,
He plucked the wounded from the battle
And took them to a healing spot.

He swooped down to rescue pilots
Who'd lost their steeds in the sea.
If he hadn't landed on the waters,
Then where would those pilots be?

He loved his family with manly strength
Sacrificing himself to meet their needs.
He cared for his children with gentle love,
And he deserves praise for his deeds!

*Continued...*

## ODE TO A MODERN-DAY KNIGHT *(continued)*

And when his soldiering work was done
And his children were all grown,
He had compassion on men in prison,
And taught them how to live on their own.

What does every little boy want?
A Hero for a Dad!
And I thank my Heavenly Father,
For that is what I have.

## WALKING

*by: Lance Corporal Forrest Lindsey*

We are walking now
Sun roaring steamy hate
Nerves are set
Metal on metal
Eyes straining
Ears hearing only the cadence and clank of our steps.

Sweat streams down our faces
Flies bite at our elbows
Ragged breath another step

A thin click -
The dirt jumps
The slam of a great steel door
Irreversibly shut
Mangling soft muscle and bone
With hopeless agony

We're walking again
Man following man
Pushing through the leaves
Straining and watching movement?

A sharp pop
The sound of a plank breaking
Life flowing
A yellow wax face
That was a friend

*Continued...*

## WALKING *(continued)*

We're walking again
Crossing a wide river
Hand over hand
A rope span

My hand slips
And I'm swept
Under the brown water
Forced
Coughing into my lungs

I'm awake now
Staring at the rhythmic
Rise and fall of your white chest
With eyes that will never close.

## HILL 55

*by: Lance Corporal Forrest R. Lindsey*

I can feel the damp air
press the back of my neck
The sound of canvas, wet and pounding
with the surges of the wind

My helmet drips
rain water down my chest
Along the top of my rifle
slung side-ways in front of me

The sounds of this hill recede
as the light fades among blowing clouds
In the distance, rumbles of thunder
or artillery flash among the moutains

We are alone here, on this hill
damp and threatened
A long way from
your laughter and light

Who were you to stay behind
leaving us wet and afraid?
Who are you to replace me
in the warmth of our home?

*Continued...*

## HILL 55 *(continued)*

We are good men, bright men
smashed into nothingness
bleeding until empty
on the top of this hill

Someday we'll leave here
Some way we'll come home
Until then we'll stare into darkness
waiting for what will come.

## FAR WIND
*by: Corporal Edward Lindsay*
*E-4 Vietnam*

Now the shouts were gone
The cry for help was in the far wind
The dead and wounded are gone,
Gone, some to return
Some never to see home again.

I hope it's not in vain
That these men gave their lives
I hope there was a meaningful
Purpose for these men
These men so young
With lives so unlived.

## DUTY/DEATH
*by: Corporal Edward Lindsay*
*E-4 Vietnam*

Duty is heavy as
A mountain therefore
To be highly desired.

Death was light as
A feather therefore
To be despised.

## RADIO CONTACT (FIRE MISSION)
*by: Corporal Edward Lindsay*
*E-4 Vietnam*

Gulf Four
Gulf Four
This is Gulf Three
Gulf Three, Gulf Four go ahead
Gulf Four, Gulf Three we have a target
Coordinates 139/261 give me one Willie Peter two H.E.
Fire at will, over
Gulf Three, Gulf Four
We have a copy, 1 W.P., 2 H.E., over
Gulf Four, Gulf Three
You're 50 yards short
Crank her up, give me 5 H.E.
Fire for effect, over
Gulf Three, Gulf Four
50 yards short, are you sure, over
Roger Gulf Four, 50 yards, crank her up, come on, over
Roger Gulf Three, 50 yards, 5 H.E.
Gulf Four, Gulf Three
You got a hit, you got a hit
Give me 5 more, moooor
G G G Gu Gulf Four
We been Hiittt
Gulf Three, this is Gulf Four
Gulf Three, this is Gulf Four, over
Gulf Three, do you copy,
Do you copy
Gulf Four to medivac
out......

## COPING
*by: Corporal Edward Lindsay*
*E-4 Vietnam*

Lying, crying, dying in a hole, baring my soul
Watching, waiting for the shell to explode
Reaching in my head, trying to understand.
Why, why I'm here, why they're here
Why man will always kill man
Why no one will try to cope.
This is a small planet, let's live together.

All we have to do is love one another,
We'll begin to discover.
The meaning is inside,
Inside you,
Inside me,
Let's be FREE!!

## WELL, CAPTAIN

*by: Corporal Edward Lindsay*
*E-4 Vietnam*

You cannot be proud Captain,
For you see.
The violence you wrought cannot be.
In the living world
Things must be true.
The war you lived
Gained nothing for you.

You died as you lived
By your own bloody hand.
Had you reached out for woman or man.
You could have been saved
From your living hell
By helping others find the well.

The well of life runs oh so deep,
You were so shallow
I never heard you speak.
I say these things now
For you see
The Captain is just a memory.

## LOST BUT NOT FORGOTTEN/MISPLACED
*by: Corporal Edward Lindsay*
*E-4 Vietnam*

I think we became bored
Or ashamed of our lives,
Or perhaps it was the rut
Of our parents existence.

At any rate, we were looking for something
To occupy our time, our life,
Trying to build a new road,
Or rebuild the old one.

White Rabbit
............Turn on, Tune in, Drop out.

California Dreamin
............Haight-Ashbury.

My Generation
............Flower Child.

For What it's Worth
............Descent, Denounce, Defiance, Demand.

Abraham, Martin and John
............Walkin Over the Hill with Bobby

2,000 Light Years from Home
............One Small Step for Man
One Giant Leap for Mankind

*Continued...*

## LOST BUT NOT FORGOTTEN/MISPLACED *(continued)*

Rainy Day Women
............Greenwich Village.

A Day in the Life
............Trying to Conceive the Everday.

Eight Miles High
............Wanting to Touch the Sky.

The Balance
............Searching for Compassion

Ball and Chain
............Searching for Love.

In-A-Gadda-Da-Vidda
............Heavy, Appealing Free.

Purple Haze
............L.S.D. Lysergic Acid Diethylamide.

Sitting on the Dock of the Bay
............Lost but Never Forgotten

Black Magic Woman
............Balanced Artistic Creation.

House of the Rising Sun
............Lonely and Used.

*Continued...*

## LOST BUT NOT FORGOTTEN/MISPLACED *(continued)*

Strawberry Fields Forever
............We Hoped They Were.

Imagine
............

A Whiter Shade of Pale
............Our Theme Song,
or Our Swan?

And then they invented Vietnam.
Maybe they thought they could get rid of us.
May they did?

# WHY

*by: Corporal Edward Lindsay*
*E-4 Vietnam*

And as we walk upon the hill,
A rifle cracks out
And another life is wasted.
Wasted in a war,
A war that no man should have to fight.

And as the chopper comes in
To pick up a life that is no more
A tear rolls down your cheek,
Again you asked yourself why.
Why, why should a life be taken,
Taken in a land
Where it's own people say
I don't care.

Maybe someday the question
Will be answered
But for now you say
Why and what for.

## THIRTEEN YEARS AFTER
*by: Corporal Edward Lindsay*
*E-4 Vietnam*

The time has come, we will prevail
Let's finish the song, let's tell the tale
Of the Vietnam War, the lives it entailed
Men will come, men will die
The sergeant's orders, I still hear him cry.

Oh, will we ever forget
The pain
On climbing up and taking aim
To slay the enemy of the day
To find that it's only a play
A play that has no end
As long as man will always pretend.

We marched on, into the night
Our thoughts on yesterday's firefight
The bullets rang out the screams and fears
It all fell dead, on innocent ears
We got back up, started to go
Those who could, the others laid low.

We walked on past, paddies and fields
On and on onto the next hill
Climbing up we couldn't see
The N.V.A. and V.C.
The feeling of death was oh so near
The response to survive was everywhere.

*Continued...*

**THIRTEEN YEARS AFTER** *(continued)*

I heard a shot, we felt the pain
Almost instantly it came again
It's hard to write the things I say
The best part of me died that day
Surviving was the winning in the war
That had no begining.

# FREEDOM HILL
*by: Corporal Edward Lindsay*
*E-4 Vietnam*

A refuge from this tormented hell
An escape from the naked reality
This farce called the Vietnam conflict
Can any one truly escape?
When you're chin deep in stark
Memories of companions
Fallen and yet to fall

Trying to ignore brutal destruction
Terrified to dwell on it for too long
Gruesome scene of a comrade
Eyes blank, staring into the unknown
Arm shredded at the elbow, crying
Trying to push guts back into a belly
Mind on the brink of insanity
War's distorted sanity

Animalism the cost of survival
Haven't bathed for weeks
Becoming acclimated to the stink
M-60 machine gun spewing death
Yet it has become your best freind
Feeling warm and natural in hand
A remarkable killing instrument

*Continued...*

## FREEDOM HILL *(continued)*

Freedom Hill, an oasis in the heated
Jungles of this hideous theatre
Hoping if you drink enough
Get drunk, numb your mind
Somehow it will all disappear
Alas, who can swallow that much pain
Eighteen-year-old toy soldiers
Old before their prime-time

Growing in the shadow of my father
The heroics of John Wayne
Coping with the illusion of
My country right or wrong
Mother, Uncle Sam and apple pie
Undeniable feelings of patriotism
Too strong to belie my call to duty
Faced now with the stench of rotting apples
Caught in a no win situation
Left to hunger for the promised glory

# OLD WOMAN
*by: Corporal Edward Lindsay*
*E-4 Vietnam*

V.C. Ravaged Village, now quiet
Men taken in the night.

Old woman, left crying
Taken young, taught to fight.

Small slimy fish-eel, caught in stream
Chopped into equal pieces.

Regarded as gourmet delight
Innards cooked, what delicacies.

Beetle-nut juice dripping
Wrinkled, numb, swollen hands.

Eyes reflecting years of strife
Fish-eel noodles, fill shallow pain.

Smoke filled bamboo hut
Barrage of N.V.A. mortar rounds.

Innocent old woman, now dead
Leaving, a hole in the ground.

## THE FIGHTING GREEN
### (Of Vietnam)
*by: Corporal N. Joseph Aquilano*
*1st Marine Division F.M.F.*
*1942-1946 World War II*

To the men in fighting green,
"The Proud, The Few, The Marines"
I salute you for the deeds you've done.
For the glory you've brought to our Corps.
The courage you've shown in jungles far,
In lands you've never seen before.
The sleepless nights, and sweating days
To find the enemy and not be his prey.
To avoid his ingenious traps he sets each day,
To outwit him at a trade he knows so well.
He'll wonder how these men in green,
Can outfight him at every scene.
He'll learn to respect a fighting Marine.
For their training they took to heart.
They cursed their D.I.'s for driving them so hard,
Under sweating sun, and burning sands,
It was their job to make boys into fighting men.
The pay off comes when the battle is done,
The D.I.'s job was well done.
We'll stand tall, one and all.
For there is no one like the fighting green.
"The Proud, The Few, The Marines"

**MG gunner, USMC 7th MEB; Al-Jubayl, August 1990**
*Artwork by Ronald Volstad*
*from Elite Series 45: US Armies of the Gulf War*
© Osprey Publishing

# GULF WAR

## (1990 - 1991)

| | |
|---|---|
| Total service members | 2,322,332 |
| Deployed to Gulf | 1,136,658 |
| Battle deaths | 148 |
| Other deaths in service (theater) | 235 |
| Other deaths in service (nontheater) | 914 |
| Nonmortal woundings | 467 |
| Living veterans (35)[1] | 1,753,530 |

1. Median ages.

*Source: Department of Defense and Veterans Administration, Sept. 30, 2001.*

## BEAUTY AND DEATH
### Brothers Tüfelhunden
*by: Fmr. Sgt. C. S. Emory*
*USMC 2/2 ed MarDiv.*
*Persian Gulf 1990-1991*

I think of children's dreams existing inside
of their smiles,
giving life a peace,
As I live through this darkness.

Humbled by your beauty,
your intelligence, your care.
This kind of love is my strength,
my rock, my self-worth.
You gave back what was lost
without your care, your compassion, your understanding.

Peace is nightmare that surrounds
those who know death, forever
smelling its odor, trying to forget.

Whenever we are separated
From one another, and apart
not hearing each other's voices.
The closer I grow towards
you, the wiser I become.

Regardless if we die in the fight,
as long as chivalry exists, as long as
those of nobility lay down their lives
for a better truth...
                    ...an unending tie will bind us...
    ...Together...
                    ...it is an honor to serve with you
        always into death.

## I DIED THERE
*by: Fmr. Sgt. C. S. Emory*
*USMC/ 2/2 ed MarDiv.*
*Persian Gulf 1990-1991*

As my thoughts wander,
to things that could happen.
My heart races,
adrenaline flows like blood.
We stand at the ready,
for the things that are to happen.
A last minute gear check,
we each shake hands and say,
"See you when the storm's over".
Turning away walking back,
I think of what might be.
Looking back only once,
I see a dense cloud over my friend...
...my brother.

That strange smoke overwhelms the evening,
on things that are to be.
Like a blanket,
darkness it comes.
Morning the command,
silently passed throughout.
We have landed,
As Marines before us,
knowing that death will be found there.
The music of artillery precedes,
as we move forward.
"Shake and bake'em" boys,
steel on target.

*Continued...*

### I DIED THERE *(continued)*

As we meet our enemies,
one thought precedes the fight.
Get home in one piece,
our minds function as one, as
rounds ring out.
Incoming! shouted,
we take a hit.
Ticked-off and now scared,
anger and fear combine.
My enemies *will* precede me,
if I am to die today.
As I protect my friend...
...my Nation.

We fix'em and feed'em,
our prisoners.
While they kill our brothers.
A young boy comes into sight, enemy,
his face is beaten.
And, yet, he sits on the stretcher,
motionless, a blackness in his eyes.
This is our enemy, his mind and heart
broken in the fight...
...what Respect he has earned.

One hundred hours in, the storm's
over...
...but my brother doesn't smile.
I returned home to,
find a war in my mind always,
A piece of me gone...
...dead inside.

## SEMPER FI
*by: Captain Thomas A. Pitt, Jr.*

Hey old man, why so spry?
What's that twinkle in your eye?
The war was barely four days old
And won in the field with battles bold.

What is it to you, your day is past
The glories of youth cannot last.
What's that you say, you were in the Corps
And the Persian Gulf becomes part of the lore.

Those brave young troops of the First and Second
Made a frontal assault at the C.G.'s beckon.
He put them in tough where he knew they'd excel
And watched in awe as the enemy fell.

'Neath the starry banner and Marine red and gold,
They went into battle with the heroes of old.
Beside the power of bomb and cannon
Was Tripoli's spirit and Lt. O'Bannon.

The ranks rose up and seemed almost fuller
As though flanks were protected by Chestey Puller
The foe gave up when they found it no rumor
That they faced the Marines of Gen. Boomer.

They all gathered round and joined in the fold
The Marines of today and the heroes of old.
Though perhaps unseen Sgt. Daily looked in
And Smedley Butler was heard over the din.

*Continued...*

### SEMPER FI *(continued)*

These Leathernecks of Globe and Anchor
Are sure to raise an enemy's rancor.
No matter the battle, no matter the war
They're always faithful to Country and Corps.

So here's to the troops of the first to fight,
The saber-toothed fang of our Country's might.
And here's to the enemy that heard over the roar
The strident brass band of Esprit de Corps.

## DESERT STORM
*by: Corporal Albert P. Husted*
*USMC "64-68"*
*Vietnam '65 & 66*

January 16, a day we'll remember well.
The day our comrades went to war
To serve their time in Hell.

As we said good-bye to the ones we love.
And watch them walk away.
We pray to God to keep them safe
And bring them home one day.

For many it will be a first
Sons and daughters alike
But with our faith in God and them
We know they'll do just fine.

What they need right now
From all of us to make it through each day,
Is to let them know we're behind them all
And support them in everyway.

We count the days one by one
As we wake to each morning sun
Thinking about our loved ones abroad
Until our day is done.

As we listen to the newsbreaks
That keep us well informed
Let us say a prayer tonight
For our troops in "Desert Storm."

*Continued...*

### DESERT STORM *(continued)*

With all of us together
No family will stand alone
And with our faith in this great land
One day we'll hear, "Mom, I'm coming home."

And while we are awaiting
For them to return that day
Let us give thanks to God in prayer
GOD BLESS THE U.S.A.

# AMERICA'S WARS TOTAL

| | |
|---|---|
| Military service during war | 42,348,460 |
| Battle deaths | 650,954 |
| Other deaths in service (theater) | 13,853 |
| Other deaths in service (nontheater) | 229,661 |
| Nonmortal woundings | 1,431,290 |
| Living war veterans | 18,865,926 |
| Living veterans | 25,038,459 |

*Source: Department of Defense and Veterans Administration, Sept. 30, 2001.*

# MISC.

## BROTHERHOOD
*by: Captain Benjamin Spieler*
*Pohang, Korea 1998*

Where they love and lie, sell and buy
They think little of us, knowing less;
We drain the dregs from their kegs
With a siren's song to loneliness;
Preserving with a creed of steel
An impossible ideal;
Following the falling star
Of things as they should be,
Not as they are.
When the sabers start to rattle
Shadows threatening the sky
Marching to the field of battle
Where the Nation's fortunes lie,
We'll unsheathe the sword of honor
Sharpened in the years of peace,
Heap our hardy prayers upon her
That her glory may increase,
Hand to her the sweet libation
Of our own devoted blood,
And on the altar of the Nation
Sacrifice our Brotherhood

## ELIANA
*by: Captain Benjamin Spieler*
*Bogota, Colombia 2001*

The carnage of leaves from the dying trees
Clothes your naked body like a bridal gown;
The gardens of starlight that blossom with snow
Light arrows of thought in your watering eyes
Like flowering diamonds in rivers of milk;
And the touch of your breath on my prison of death
Is like wind on an eggshell of dust.

## THE LION OF JUDAH
*by: Captain Benjamin Spieler*
*Cape Town, South Africa 1999*

Like an orphan of the mountains
From a crest of bone
He fastens the Necklace of Disaster
That hangs from the stars
Round the Gullet of Morning.

He mines the spine of steel
For billows of broken water
Whose coral curls rustle
In the cavities of light
Like locks on the Lion of Judah

## LIKE RANDOM DROPS OF HEAVEN'S BLOOD
*by: Captain Benjamin Spieler*
*Puerto Rosario, Paraguay 1999*

Like random drops of Heaven's blood
On your face descends
The Shadow of the Hand of God
Five great fingers of crimson light
Caressing the orb of the sun.
The sifting waters of the rune lake envelope you,
The flames of your thought shriek in colossal bird-tones-
Fling your body into the light of me,
All sinew and bone of it,
Cling with paper arms to the sight of me
And as we watch the blood course in
Your translucent skin
Our base laughter shall devour the high flame.

# ABADDON
*by: Captain Benjamin Spieler*
*Lagos, Nigeria 1999*

The sun beats the sky like a bloody fist
Over boiling seas of amethyst
Showering beads of crimson light
Like random drops of Heaven's blood
From the whirlwind of the open wound
To the siphons of our hollow minds.
Our digits tickle the wavering atoms
Like slugs whose lazy locomotion
Excites a rhythmic Armagedd'
On the quivering strings of a violin.
Disintegrating by inches
Feeding love to flesh-eating flowers
We mutate into majestic Abaddon
Fluttering like wind-swept origami
Until our tired wings collapsing
Tumble into corrosive foam.
We peer through embrasures at promiscuous shadows
Under the silver veil of Orion:
So easy the cast of culture cracks;
Under a thimble of restraint
Yearning minds are stifled
Like a pillow over the mouth of God.
Like poison, like disease
At the absence of Love's arrival
Our desperation bestows
Only internal echoes
And maudlin memories.

## THE SEEKER
*by: Captain Benjamin Spieler*
*Written on the USS Fort McHenry*
*in the East China Sea 1998*

Above the moors the thunder roars
And waters lap the lonely shores
With empty sighs like lullabies
Whispered over lidded eyes.
A wind is rising from the south
And issues as if from a mouth
That breathes a low and plaintive psalm.
The Holy word is scarcely heard
But flutters lightly like a bird
Released at last by lonely hand
To seek a solitary land
And settle there above the flood
Awash in waves of human blood.
Now from this makeshift raft I see
The pillars of eternity
One in darkness, one in dawn
Where sunlight rests upon the crests
Of waves that roll forever on.
Human spirits upward fly
Their fingers scratch the iron sky
Some want to live, some want to die
But those who fight against their fate
More rapidly evaporate
And all their passion and their pain
Descends again in tears like rain.
Still I seek for Adonai
Between the waters and the sky
Through the darkness toward the dawn
Where sunlight rests upon the crests
Of waves that roll forever on.

## MY FLESH SHALL NOT DEFEAT ME
*by: Captain Benjamin Spieler*
*Written on the USS Fort McHenry*
*in the East China Sea, 1998*

They shall not defeat me, these sins of lust
Though I grapple and gasp in the grip of the grave
As a mill grinds grain I shall grind them to dust
Though they curdle my blood till the sun stand still
I shall grind them to dust in the wheel of my will
    And my flesh shall not defeat me.

They shall not defeat me, these limbs like stalks
That twist in the wind when my spirit walks
Let them twist in the wind till their twisting's done
Though they blot out the light of the blinking sun
    I'll run my race till the race is run
    And my flesh shall not defeat me.

It shall not defeat me, this fear of death
That whispers words like shibboleth
Though all is lost that I hoped to save
And I grapple and gasp in the grip of the grave
I won't shiver and shudder and cry aloud
For pain shall pass like a passing cloud
No fear can stain a soldier's shroud
    So my flesh shall not defeat me.

It shall not defeat me, this flesh of mine
For flesh is lost in the flood of time
Though flesh and body and blood rebel
A man is free though he cannot tell
Till he wander in Heaven or wallow in Hell
    So my flesh shall not defeat me.

## TRANSLATION OF PSALM 126
*by: Captain Benjamin Spieler*
*Translated in Jacmel, Haiti in 1997*

By the waters of Babylon we lay down and wept
When we remembered thee, O Zion;
In the heart of the city
We looped our lyres on the limbs of the willows
For the throng that destroyed us demanded a song,
They who mocked us demanded our mirth, saying,
"Sing a song of Zion!"
How here can we utter a lay of the Lord in a land of calamity?
If I forget thee, O Jerusalem, let my right hand lose its art,
Let my tongue cleave to my palate if I loose thee from my heart,
If I labor not for Jerusalem as a love apart.
Remember their evils on the Children of Edom, O Lord,
The day they flayed the face of our city with their sword:
O ill-destined daughter of Babylon, blessed is the one
Who renders thy deserts for the evils thou hast done!
Blessed, who waters the rocks with the blood of thy son.

## THE NEW NAVY, 1999
*by: Captain Benjamin Spieler*
*Written aboard the USS Carter Hall*
*in the Atlantic, 1999*

We're riders on a ship of fools
Adrift on angry seas
Measuring her madness
In latitude degrees.
Her helmsman is a harlequin
Her officers are whores
Her engines take testosterone
But mermaids man the oars.
No alcohol has made them drunk
No liquor fills their veins
But women reel from bunk to bunk
Aroused by labor pains.
And if the Admiral orders her
Into contested seas
She'll give a shout and, turning about,
Seduce our enemies.

## TAMERLANE

*by: Captain Benjamin Spieler*
*Port-au-Prince, Haiti 1997*

Then Tamerlane stripped off the skin of his innocence
And lay where the skeletons scavenge the corn from the cradles of August
Where the orb of all-radiance hangs from the limbs of a withering tree
And delivers like lightning as far as forever perpetual shadow.
He fashioned a raft from the worm-eaten wood of the withering tree
Pointing its prow through the wandering wind with a sail of skin
That twisted and turned like a heretic burned in the flame of Salvation.
He followed the flight of the Daughter of Water as far as forever
Till bright as a star on the axle of evening her lips of desire
Covered the sun as it fled toward tomorrow with kisses of fire.
Then Tamerlane wept like a flesh-eating flower devoured by hunger
While bright as a star on the axle of evening the Daughter of Water
Danced like a dancer who dances with Death in a circle of slaughter-
Brighter than stars on the axle of evening her lips of desire
Covered the sun as it fled toward tomorow with kisses of fire.
From the rocks by the shores of the River Shavuot rose Voices of Sorrow
That cried to the Children of Adam aloud through their curtains of horror:
"Silence governs the tongue of Heaven
Of stars that night have been loved ones' eyes
Long past, long past they have wept their clouds
Long past, before having loosed the shrouds
That shivered the Heavens and severed the shadows
That forgave us forgetting forgotten truths
On a highway as wide as a river of life
But as livid and raw as a wound."
Now the Daughter of Water arises alive
From a whirlwind of wave on her glistening shell

*Continued...*

## TAMERLANE *(continued)*

Avowing the law that no freedom of Heaven
Surpasses the pleasure of prison in Hell;
From the lap of the lake with a loping gait
She cripples the flower, harasses the sun
With her nipples inviolate molded and milked
By the arm of the earth with a razor of skill
She suckled her lovers with flashing rain:
Transfixed by the poles of the lonesome sky
Spiralling upward like swimmers to surface
They swallow her mists of immortal ether.
Rolling her cataracts heavenward under
Birds that bellow litanies of thunder
She spatters saliva on their livid faces
And her tears of brine
And with a great French kiss embraces
The Capitoline.

# A PRIMITIVE PRAYER
*by: Captain Benjamin Spieler*
*Bogota, Colombia in 2001*

Our age is like some creeping thing
Endowed with neither hoof nor wing
But ignorant of nature's laws
It motivates with metal claws.
Now glib seductive bitter crass
Like Beauty sepulchered in glass
I pity her remote and sad
Imprisoned in a perfume ad
Patron Goddess of the city
Our souls reflected in her stare
Blank, but eager for publicity
Stamped on a billboard in Times Square.
Quarantined in ivory tower
Palisades are more than prison
Sands of time dissolve my power
Dull the dagger of decision
Elsewhere joys of love and laughter
Run before and linger after
Whose cadence soft and rhythmic measure
Bind in manacles of pleasure.
Alas I cannot conjure up
A demon from a golden cup
Nor throw a serpent from a rod
Nor hold a mirror up to God
But merely tremble in the light
A hesitating sybarite.
In this attic of the ages

*Continued...*

## A PRIMITIVE PRAYER *(continued)*

Terror hangs like rotting meat
Around my walls a battle rages
In a desert of deceit
Opposing armies line the river
Flowing through the fertile plain
The holy river runs forever
Spilling like an opened vein.
Where is the sun whose violet rays
Alone can heal us of our pain?
We wander in a twilight haze
While Heaven showers crimson rain.
But God shall weigh us in his scales
On the day when daylight fails
Unborn generations slain
Shall walk the cities of the plain
And fill the citadels of bronze
With choruses of holy songs.
And Love shall hold me in her sway
When the daylight fails the day
And lead me broken to her home
Underneath the starry dome
To heal the fragments of my heart
By prayer more primitive than art.

# UNKNOWN
# AUTHORS

**FRIEND IN NEED**
*Submitted by: Corporal Tim J. Mayhew*

To our village yesterday
Came a man from far away
Always laughing very bold
Though he looks not very old.
Got the V.C. on the run
Killed some with the machine gun
Dressed in green instead of black
Carries children on his back;
When they ask what the emblem means,
He says "The United States Marines".

In case of trouble, day or night,
He's always ready for a fight
Ask for help, he says, "Can Do"
Makes damn fine ambush, too.
Tried to learn a Vietnam word:
"Sari bao tat" all we heard.
What this means, we do not know
Nor why he often talks of "Snow"
Tall and strong, hard and lean,
He's one tough U.S. Marine.

He guards our village, front to rear,
We do our tasks and feel no fear.
Cong no longer raid at night,
Children sleep and grow up right.
No more torture, no more danger,
No more taxes paid to strangers.
He teaches us courage, teaches pride,
"Face your trouble, do not hide".
We build to make our land serene,
Thanks to the fine U.S. Marine.

## G.I. PROTEST
*Submitted by: Corporal Tim J. Mayhew*

Take a man, put him alone,
Put him 12,000 miles from his home.
Empty his heart of all but blood,
Make him live in sweat and mud.
This is the life I have to live,
And why my soul to the devil I give.

You sit at home in your easy chairs,
Not knowing what it's like being over here.
You have a ball without near trying,
While over here your son is dying.

You burn your draft cards, march at dawn,
Plant your signs on the Whitehouse lawn.
You all try to ban the bomb,
There's no war in Vietnam.

Use your drugs, have your fun,
Then refuse to use the gun.
There's nothing left for you to do,
And I'm supposed to die for you.

I'll hate you till the day I die,
You make me hear my buddy cry.
I saw his arm a bloody shred,
I heard them say, "this one is dead".

*Continued...*

### G.I. PROTEST *(continued)*

It's a damn large price to have to pay,
So that you can live another day.
He had the guts to fight and die,
He paid the price, But what did he buy?

He brought you life by losing his,
But who gives a damn what a MARINE gives.
His wife, his parents, and his sons,
But they're the only ones.

## BURY ME WITH MARINES
*Submitted by: Bob Chester, Sr.*

I've played a lot of roles in life;
I've met a lot of men.
I've done a lot of things
I'd like to think I wouldn't do again.

And though I'm young, I'm old enough
To know someday I'll die.
And to think about what lies beyond,
Beside whom I would lie.

Perhaps it doesn't matter much;
Still if I had my choice.
I'd want a grave 'mongst Marines when,
At least death quells my voice.

I'm sick of the hypocrisy,
Of lectures of the wise.
I'll take the man, with all the flaws,
Who goes, though scared, and dies.

The troops I knew were common men;
They didn't want the war;
They fought because their fathers and
Their fathers had before.

*Continued...*

## BURY ME WITH MARINES *(continued)*

They cursed and killed and wept;
God knows...they're easy to deride.
But bury me with men like these;
They faced the guns and died.

It's funny when you think of it,
The way we got along.
We'd come from different worlds
To live in one where no one belongs.

I didn't even like them all;
I'm sure they'd all agree.
Yet I would give my life for them,
I know some did for me.

So bury me with Marines, please,
Though much maligned they be.
Yes, bury me with Marines,
For I miss their company.

We'll not soon see their likes again;
We've had our fill of war.
But bury me with men like them,
Till someone else does more.

## THIS IS MY RIFLE
*Submitted by: Bob Chester, Sr.*

Do you wonder why that rifle,
Is hanging in my den?
You know I rarely take it down,
But I touch it now and then.

It's rather slow and heavy,
By standards of today.
But not too many years ago,
It swept the rest away.

It's held its own in battles,
Through snow, or rain, or sun.
And I had one just like it,
This treasured old M-1.

It went ashore at Bougainville,
In Nineteen Forty-Three.
It stormed the beach at Tarawa,
Through a bullet-riddled sea.

Saipan knew its strident bark,
Kwajelein, its sting.
The rocky caves of Peleliu,
Resounded with its ring.

*Continued...*

**THIS IS MY RIFLE** *(continued)*

It climbed the hill on Iwo,
With men who wouldn't stop.
And left our nation's banner,
Flying on the top.

It poked its nose in Pusan,
Screamed an angry roar.
And took the First Division,
From Chosin Reservoir.

Well, time moves on,
And things improve,
With rifles and with men.
And that is why the two of us,
Are sitting in my den.

But sometimes on a winter night,
While thinking of my Corps.
I know that if the bugle blew,
We'd be a team once more.

## UNKNOWN TITLE
*Submitted by: Bob Chester, Sr.*

He was gettng old and paunchy
And his hair was falling fast,
And he sat around the Legion,
Telling stories of the past.

Of a war that he once fought in
And the deeds that he had done,
In his exploits with his buddies;
They were heroes, every one.

And 'tho sometimes to his neighbors
His talks became a joke,
All his buddies listened quietly
For they knew where of he spoke.

But we'll hear his tales no longer,
For ol' Bob has passed away,
And the world's a little poorer
For a Soldier died today.

He won't be mourned by many,
Just his children and his wife.
For he lived an ordinary,
Very quiet sort of life.

*Continued...*

**UNKNOWN TITLE** *(continued)*

He held a job and raised a family,
Going quietly on his way;
And the world won't note his passing,
''Tho a Soldier died today'.

When politicians leave this earth,
Their bodies lie in state,
While thousands note their passing,
And proclaim that they were great.

Papers tell of their life stories
From the time that they were young
But the passing of a Soldier
Goes unnoticed, and unsung.

Is the greatest contribution
To the welfare of our land,
Some jerk who breaks his promise
And cons his fellow man?

Or the ordinary fellow
Who in times of war and strife,
Goes off to serve his country
And offers up his life?

The politician's stipend
And the style in which he lives,
Are often disproportionate,
To the service that he gives.

*Continued...*

### UNKNOWN TITLE *(continued)*

While the ordinary Soldier,
Who offered up his all,
Is paid off with a medal
And perhaps a pension, small.

It's so easy to forget them,
For it is so many times
That our Bobs and Jims and Johnnys,
Went to battle, but we know.

It is not the politicians
With their compromise and ploys,
Who won for us the freedom
That our country now enjoys.

Should you find yourself in danger,
With your enemies at hand,
Would you really want some cop-out,
With his ever waffling stand?

Or would you want a Soldier—
His home, his country, his kin,
Just a common Soldier,
Who would fight until the end.

He was just a common Soldier,
And his ranks are growing thin,
But his presence should remind us
We may need his like again.

*Continued...*

**UNKNOWN TITLE** *(continued)*

For when countries are in conflict,
We find the Soldier's part
Is to clean up all the troubles
That the politicians start.

If we cannot do him honor
While he's here to hear the praise,
Then at least let's give him homage
At the ending of his days.

Perhaps just a simply headline
In the paper that might say:

**"OUR COUNTRY IS IN MOURNING,
A SOLDIER DIED TODAY."**

## MY DARKNESS
*Submitted by: Bob Chester, Sr.*

The darkness held such hidden terror
Far beneath the sun above.
For my own safety I did not care,
For what I had to do, there was no love.

Small dark tunnels leading everywhere...
A maze in which to crawl...
Not knowing who was waiting there,
Or if the earth above would fall...

I could not hesitate, or even think.
I went to seek, to find, to destroy and to do.
The unexpected can happen in a blink of an eye...
My job was done by such a few...

It's over now, except for the dreams and memory.
At night it haunts me still, with the smell of explosive powder
And the taste of damp dirt in my mouth.
And yet it's part of me, it had to be...

Forget the smells, the fears, and dark and the blood from
Self and adversary...
The job of a Tunnel Rat is not a lark.
So long ago, yet I am still wary...

*Continued...*

## MY DARKNESS *(continued)*

As I close my eyes at night the memories return.
I wake into the darkness of my room, my body in a cold sweat.
From the dreams I had just left.
My hands over my face I stand and start to pace and
Think to myself, will this horror ever end.
Will I have to die to find the peace I seek?
From deep within I feel that I must go on and grit
My teeth with zeal.
The question comes again into my mind will I always live
In the darkness of the tunnels and never see the light?
I must keep up the fight and continue to walk toward the light.

## TWAS THE NIGHT BEFORE CHRISTMAS, AND ALL THROUGH THE SKIES
### *Submitted by: Bob Chester, Sr.*

Air defenses were up, with electronic eyes.
Combat pilots were nestled in ready-room beds,
As enemy silhouettes danced in their heads.

Every jet on the apron, each SAM in its tube,
Was triply-redundant linked to the Blue Cube,
And ELINT and AWACS gave coverage so dense
That nothing that flew could slip through our defense.

When out of the klaxon arose such a clatter
I dashed to the screen to see what was the matter;
I dialed up the gain and then quick as a flash
Fine-adjusted the filters to damp out the hash.

And there found the source of the warning we'd heeded:
An incoming blip, by eight escorts preceded.
"Alert status red!" went the word down the wire,
As we gave every system the codes that meant "FIRE"!

On Aegis! Up Patriot, Phalanx and Hawk!
And scramble our fighters—let's send the whole flock!
Launch decoys and missiles! Use chaff by the yard!
Get the kitchen sink up! Call the National Guard!

*Continued...*

## TWAS THE NIGHT BEFORE CHRISTMAS,
## AND ALL THROUGH THE SKIES *(continued)*

They turned toward the target, moved toward it, converged.
Till the tracks on the radar all finally merged,
And the sky was lit up with a demonic light,
As the foe became pieces in the high arctic night.

So we sent out some recon to look for debris,
Yet all that they found, both on land and on sea,
Were some toys, a red hat, a charred left leather boot,
Broken sleighbells, some gloves, and a ripped parachute.

Now it isn't quite Christmas, with Saint Nick shot down.
There are unhappy kids in each village and town.
Can the Spirit of Christmas even hope to evade
All the web of defenses we've carefully made?

Just look how the gadgets we use to protect us
In other ways alter, transform, and affect us.
They can keep us from things that make life more worth living,
Like love for each other, and thoughts of just giving.

But a crash program's on: Working hard, night and day,
All the elves are constructing a radar-proof sleigh.
So let's wait for next Christmas, in cheer and in health,
And be good boys and girls, as Santa goes STEALTH

## A CHRISTMAS POEM FOR MARINES
*Submitted by: Bob Chester, Sr.*

'Twas the night before Christmas, the stars shining bright,
The sentry was walking, his left, then his right.

His rifle it swung from his shoulder with ease,
His head kept alert from a chill in the breeze.

The troops were all nestled and warm in their racks,
While he stood his duty, his feet making tracks.

For he, in his helmet, with his rifle at side,
Had just settled down in that 12 to 4 stride.

Then what to the shock of the sentry appeared,
Was a little green sleigh pulled by camouflaged deer,
With a little old driver in dress blues and sword.

The sentry just stood there not saying a word,
He watched in amazement with eyes all aglow,
As the reindeer, in silence, pulled the sleigh low.

With a wink from the driver, a tip from his cover,
The sleigh like a Huey, just pulled up and hovered.

The sentry was startled, bewitched, and in doubt,
But duty prevailed and these words rang out.
"Now wait a minute—halt who goes there!?

*Continued...*

## A CHRISTMAS POEM FOR MARINES *(continued)*

But the little man smiled, "you've nothing to fear,
For as sure as it's Christmas, and as sure as you're here,
I've stopped on my route just to bring you good cheer!"

"Now attention to orders!" he said with a flair.
Then read from a page that he held in the air:

"For attention to duty while walking your post,
On the day of the year that we cherish the most,
Here in this place on this solemn occasion,
I thank you, Marine, on behalf of the nation!"

He saluted the sentry, and cut sharp and clear,
Then he took up the reins as he called to his deer,
"On Belleau, on Iwo, on An-Hoa and Chosin,
On you named for places both hell-hot and frozen!"

And he called out once more as he sped out of sight,
Merry Christmas, Marines, carry on and good night!"

SEMPER FIDELIS

## UNKNOWN TITLE
*Submitted by: Bob Chester, Sr.*

Bless em all, bless em all,
The Commies, the U.N. and all;
Those slant-eyed Chink soldiers
Struck Hagaru-ri
And now know the meaning of U.S.M.C.
But we're saying goodbye to them all,
We're Harry's police force on call.
So put back your pack on,
The next step is Saigon,
Cheer up, me lads, bless em all!

## PRAYER FOR A MARINE
*Submitted by: Robert Andrews*

Lord, shadow with your Loving care,
The path of this Marine
On land, on sea, by night, by day
From him all dangers seen.
The Leathernecks of God, brave men
The soldiers of the sea.
Wherever peril threatens most,
Marines will always be.
Be with them Lord, in all the lands
Where duty bids them go.
Keep strong their faith, keep high their Hearts.
Protect them from the foe
–AMEN–

## 'TWAS THE NIGHT BEFORE CHRISTMAS
## WITH A TWIST
*Submitted by: Harold Siegel*

'Twas the night before Christmas,
He lived all alone.
In a one bedroom house made of
Plaster and stone.

I had come down the chimney
With presents to give.
And to see just who
In this home did live.

I looked all about,
A strange sight I did see.
No tinsel, no presents.
Not even a tree.

No stocking by mantle,
Just boots filled with sand.
On the wall hung pictures
Of far distant lands.

With medals and badges,
Awards of all kinds.
A sober thought
Came through my mind.

*Continued...*

## 'TWAS THE NIGHT BEFORE CHRISTMAS
## WITH A TWIST *(continued)*

For this house was different,
It was dark and dreary.
I found the home of a soldier,
Once I could see clearly.

The soldier lay sleeping,
Silent, alone.
Curled up on the floor
In this one bedroom home.

The face was so gentle.
The room in such disorder.
Not how I pictured
A United States soldier.

Was this the Hero
Of whom I'd just read?
Curled up on a poncho,
The floor for a bed?

I realized the families
That I saw this night.
Owed their lives to these soldiers
Who were willing to fight.

*Continued...*

## 'TWAS THE NIGHT BEFORE CHRISTMAS
## WITH A TWIST *(continued)*

Soon "round the world.
The children would play.
And grownups would celebrate
A bright Christmas day.

They all enjoyed freedom
Each month of the year.
Because of the soliders,
Like the one lying here.

I couldn't help wonder
How many lay alone.
On a cold Christmas Eve
In a land far from home.

The very thought
Brought a tear to my eye.
I dropped to my knees
And started to cry.

The soldier awakened
And I heard a rough voice.
"Santa don't cry,
This life is my choice.

*Continued...*

## 'TWAS THE NIGHT BEFORE CHRISTMAS
## WITH A TWIST *(continued)*

I fight for freedom,
I don't ask for more.
My life is my God,
My country, my corps."

The soldier rolled over
And drifted to sleep.
I couldn't control it,
I continued to weep.

I kept watch for hours,
So silent and still.
And we both shivered
From the cold night's chill.

I didn't want to leave
On that cold, dark, night.
This guardian of honor
So willing to fight.

Then the solider rolled over,
With a voice soft and pure.
Whispered, "carry on Santa,
It's Christmas day, all is secure."

One look at my watch,
And I knew he was right.
"Merry Christmas my friend,
And to all a good night."

## A SOLDIER'S CHRISTMAS

The embers glowed softly, and in their dim light,
I gazed round the room and I cherished the sight.
My wife was asleep, her head on my chest,
My daugther beside me, angelic in rest.

Outside the snow fell, a blanket of white,
Transforming the yard to a winter delight.
The sparkling lights in the tree, I believe,
Completed the magic that was Christmas Eve.

My eyelids were heavy, my breathing was deep,
Secure and surrounded by love I would sleep
In perfect contentment, or so it would seem.
So I slumbered, perhaps I started to dream.

The sound wasn't loud, and it wasn't too near,
But I opened my eye when it tickled my ear.
Perhaps just a cough, I didn't quite know,
Then the sure sound of footsteps outside in the snow.

My soul gave a tremble, I struggled to hear,
And I crept to the door just to see who was near.
Standing out in the cold and the dark of the night,
A lone figure stood, his face weary and tight.

A solider, I puzzled, some twenty years old
Perhaps a Marine, huddled here in the cold.
Alone in the dark, he looked up and smiled,
Standing watch over me, and my wife and my child.

*Continued...*

## A SOLDIER'S CHRISTMAS *(continued)*

"What are you doing?" I asked without fear
"Come in this moment, it's freezing out here!
Put down your pack, brush the snow from your sleeve,
You should be at home on a cold Christmas Eve!"

For barely a moment I saw his eyes shift,
Away from the cold and the snow blown in drifts,
To the window that danced with a warm fire's light
Then he sighed and he said "Its really all right,
I'm out here by choice. I'm here every night."

"It's my duty to stand at the front of the line,
That separates you from the darkest of times.
No one had to ask or beg or implore me,
I'm proud to stand here like my fathers before me.

My Gramps died at 'Pearl on a day in December,'
Then he sighed, "That's a Christmas 'Gram always remembers."
My dad stood his watch in the jungles of 'Nam
And now it is my turn and so, here I am.

I've not seen my own son in more than a while,
Buy my wife sends me pictures, he's sure got her smile.
Then he bent and he carefully pulled from his bag,
The red white and blue...an American flag.

*Continued...*

## A SOLDIER'S CHRISTMAS *(continued)*

"I can live through the cold and the being alone,
Away from my family, my house and my home,
I can stand at my post through the rain and the sleet,
I can sleep in a foxhole with little to eat,
I can carry the weight of killing another
Or lay down my life with my sisters and brothers
Who stand at the front against any and all,
To insure for all time that this flag will not fall."

"So go back inside," he said, "harbor no fright
Your family is waiting and I'll be all right."
"But isn't there something I can do, at the least,
"Give you money," I asked, "or prepare you a feast?
It seems all too little for all that you've done,
For being away from your wife and your son."

Then his eye welled a tear that held no regret,
"Just tell us you love us, and never forget
To fight for our rights back at home while we're gone.
To stand your own watch, no matter how long.

For when we come home, either standing or dead,
To know you remember we fought and we bled
Is payment enough, and with that we will trust
That we mattered to you as you mattered to us.

## A YEAR OR A LIFETIME
*Submitted by: Lance Corporal Louis Cusumano*

We are the men who stand alone,
Twelve thousand miles away from home.
Our hearts are empty of all but blood,
Our bodies are covered with sweat & mud.
This is the life we chose to live,
A year or a lifetime is what we'll give.
You'll never know what it's like here.
You with your parties, girls, & beer.
Have a ball without half trying,
While over there men are dying.
Burn your draft cards or a march at dawn,
Plant your signs on the White House lawn.
Shout "Ban the Bomb"
And there is no war in Vietnam.
Pop some pills, roll in the sun
Simply refuse to carry a gun.
There is nothing else for you to do,
And I'm supposed to die for you?

## "D"—"DOG" COMPANY
*2nd Battalion, 5th Mairnes*
*Korea, July 1951*
*Overlooking the Great Punch Bowl*

*Submitted by: Robert Andrews*


*The song of "D" Company*
*(Tune of "Always")*


We'll be on the ground, always,
We are here to stay always,
It is plain to see,
We're "Dog" Company
We'll be on high ground always, always.


"Easy" Company, low ground,
And "Fox" Company no ground
It is plain to see
"Dog" makes history
We'll be on high ground, always.


Now we're on hill nine-o-seven,
That's the closest one to heaven,
We watch clouds roll by,
Planes can't fly that high,
We're highest in the sky always.

*Continued...*

### "D"—"DOG" COMPANY *(continued)*

When there is a hill to soften
"Easy" gets reserve often,
When it's too hard for "Fox"
"Dog" gets all the knocks,
We'll be climbing hills, always.

We get a patrol, all day,
Chink throws mortor shells our way,
"Easy's" in the rear
Drinking all the beer,
We get it in the rear, always.

I joined the Marine Corps one day,
I am in Korea-next day,
I'm in "Dog" Company,
That's the place for me
So I'll climb these hills, always.

The rotation plan started,
I was bumped and broken-hearted,
Somebody bumped me
So it's plain to see,
Rotation's not for me, not always.

# UNKNOWN USMC
*Submitted by: Bob Chester, Sr.*

The Chaplain wore no helmet
His head was bowed in prayer
His face was seamed with sorrow
But a trace of hope was there.

Our ranks were hushed and silent
And diminished by our loss
At our feet, the rows of crosses
Told how much the battle cost.

Rows of neat white crosses
And Stars of David too
Marked the gravesites of our brothers
Whose fighting days were through.

Friends of mine were lying there
Ski and Ace and Slim
Bo and Jack, Bill and Joe
Dusty, Tex and Jim.

Each had his simple marker
But the closest one to me
Was a plain white, wooden headboard
Marked "Unknown USMC."

*Continued...*

**UNKNOWN USMC** *(continued)*

In this final camp of comrades
It was somehow strange and odd
That a man should lie among them
Known only to his God.

Who can he be, I wondered
Was he white or black or red?
This man who shares a resting place
With our loved and honored dead.

He cannot be a stranger
But a friend whose lonely track
Has brought him here among us
I think I'll call him "Mac."

"Mac" is a name we've often used
and it's been used on me
It's better than the epitaph
"Unknown USMC."

So many times I've heard it
In the blackness of the night
Through the swirling mist of combat
With the battle at it's height.

"Hey Mac", a voice would call
We could use some help out here
I've got a man that's wounded
Can you help him to the rear?

*Continued...*

## UNKNOWN USMC *(continued)*

"Hey Mac" I'm really burning up
The sun's so blazing hot—
Can you spare a drop of water—
"Gee, thanks Mac, thanks a lot."

The day when I was wounded
Hurt and lying in the snow
A cigarette was offered me
By a man I didn't know.

He quickly stopped the bleeding
And rolled me on my back
Grinned and gripped his rifle
And said "Take it easy Mac."

A simple word, a simple name
But, still it proves to me
That no man ever really is
"Unknown USMC."

The Chaplain's prayer is finished
Our colors gently dip
The rifle squad is ready
The bugler wets his lip.

With blurry eyes and saddened heart
I heard the rifles crack
Taps floated softly in the air...
And I said goodbye to "Mac."

SEMPER FIDELIS

# SYNOPSIS OF THE AUTHORS

## Robert de Castro

He left college to serve in Korea with 1st and 11th regiments of the 1st Marine Division from December 1950 through January 1952 as a radio operator and driver. He completed college after discharge and began a career in education as a classroom teacher. After earning graduate degrees from Rutgers and Purdue, he taught economics at Montclair (NJ) State University where he was also Executive Director of the State Council on Economic Education. He retired in 1988 from an administrative position with the New Jersey State Department of Education. He now lives in Bridgewater with wife Linda.

## Master Sergeant Carl M. (Bud) DeVere, Sr. USMC

Born in St. Peter, MN August 2, 1923. Traveled with my father's circus until 1938. Met my future wife Estelle in 1938 in South Dakota. I joined the Marines in 1942, served overseas at Guadalcanal with a dive bomber squadron until February 1944. Married Estelle April 8, 1944. We had 4 children. The oldest, a boy, joined the Marines in 1968, and served in Vietnam. I served in Korea in the early 1950s with heavy artillery. During Vietnam I served with Leatherneck magazine. I retired from the Corps in 1968, and worked for the Marine Corps Museum for another 20 years.

## Sergeant George W. Henley

I graduated from High School in Pocahontas, Ark. in 1942. I had signed up for the Marines on December 8, 1941 but couldn't go on active duty until 1943 due to my age. I served in the Corp from 1943 thru 1954—three hitches from the Marshall Islands thru Korea. In the Marshall Islands, I flew as an enlisted pilot, on Guam as a stretcher bearer and with the tanks in Korea. When I got back my luck was still with me as I met Carol, my wife and we have had 51 good years together.

## John T. Maxwell, III

John T. Maxwell, III, is the proud son of a Marine. John T. Maxwell, Jr. enlisted in the Marine Corps in 1952, returned from Korea to attend Flight School, and received his wings in 1956. He served in Vietnam 1966-67 with Helicopter Squadron HMM 265. He flew 250 missions and was awarded 4 decorations for heroic achievement including the Distinguished Flying Cross. He was also awarded 3 decorations for meritorious achievement including the Navy Commendation for Achievement for the development of a program for the high speed low level delivery of emergency supplies by paradrop.

## Corporal John J. McLeod

I entered the Marine Corps in February, 1943, and attended Boot Camp at Parris Island, then to Camp LeJuene in North Carolina. After a time at Camp LeJuene, I went on a troop train across the States and into California. Then on a troop ship to the South Pacific to the Island of Pavuvu in the Solomon Islands. In 1945, we were ready for the invasion of Okinawa. In October we were ordered to China. I spent six months there, then came back to the States where I had the right amount of points to be discharged. I traveled to Bainbridge, Maryland, and received my discharge on April 7, 1946 with the rank of Corporal.

## Charles G. Monnett, Jr.

He enlisted in the Marine Corps on November 12, 1942. Started the V-12 training program at Duke University in July, 1943. Attended Boot Camp in January, 1944. Graduated from Officer Candidate School in September, 1944. Landed on Okinawa on April 1, 1945. Served as a Platoon Leader with the 29th Regiment. Trained with the Sixth Division on Guam for the invasion of Japan. In September, 1945, the Division went to Tsingtao, China for the surrender and repatriation of the Japanese. In China, he graduated from Special Services School and became Regimental Education Officer of the 22nd Marines.

## John Brinkley Moullette

Retired corporate trainer, consultant; b. Camden, N.J., Jan. 23, 1927; s. Clarence Earle Moullette and Margaret Dorothea Phillipsen. BEd, Trenton (N.J.) State Coll., 1957; MEd, Rutgers U., 1966, EdD, 1970. Cert. vocat.-tech. inst. adminstr., N.J. Instr. tech. writing Salem County Tech. Inst., Penns Grove, N.J., 1961-65; supr. vocat. edn. N.J. State Dept. Edn., Trenton, 1965-66; lectr. in edn. Rutgers U., New Brunswick, N.J., 1966-70; assoc. prof. Wash. State U., Pullman, 1970-71; rsch. prof. Ohio State U., Columbus, 1971-75; mgr. proposal devel. Telemedia, Inc., Chgo., 1975-77; mgr. edn. and tng. Royal Saudi Naval Forces, Dammam, 1977-79; mgmt. and profl, trainer Saudi Aramco, Dhahran, Saudi Arabia, 1980-89, ret. Saudi Arabia, 1989. Cons. Royal Saudi Naval Forces naval tech. tng. facilities, Dammam, Saudi Arabia, 1990-91, tng. ship Tarpon Springs, Fla., 1991-93, UN Devel. Program, Internat. Labor Orgn. Nat. Tng. Secretariat, Phnom Penh, Kingdom of Cambodia, 1993-94, Mil. Sea Lift Command USNS Comfort, 1996. Sgt. USMC, 1944-46, PTO, 1950-52, Korea; quartermaster/boatswain U.S. Micht. Marine, 1946-49. Recipient Disting. Svc. award Grad. Sch. Edn., Rutgers U., New Brunswick, 1992. Mem.: Am. Legion (comdr. China Post #1, Dhahran 1986, 1988), Phi Delta Kappa, Epsilon Pi Tau.

## Captain Thomas A. Pitt, Jr.

Westchester, PA; USMCR; Helicopter Pilot Mag. 26; Age: 69; Lawyer and retired trial judge.

## Robert Wirth, Sr.

Born on July 3, 1930, Scranton, PA. Moved to Baltimore, MD. 1941. Finished high school and some college. Joined Marine Corp. Reserve 1949. Served in Korea 1950-1951. Discharged 1952. Worked 24 years for ASARCO Inc., and 15 years for Md. Chicken Co. before retiring in 1992. Am a member of The American Legion, Maryland Korean Veterans, 1st Marine Division Assoc., The Chosin Few, and an active member for over 30 years in the Veterans of Foreign Wars. Married to wife Jean, for 50 years. Have 4 children, 5 grand children and 9 great grand children. Still write poetry on occasion for my own pleasure.

CPSIA information can be obtained at www.ICGtesting.com
234697LV00002B/23/P